IGCSE and O Level

Computer Studies
and Information Technology

IGCSE and O Level

Computer Studies
and Information Technology

Chris Leadbetter and Stewart Wainwright

CAMBRIDGE UNIVERSITY PRESS

Cambridge, New York, Melbourne, Madrid, Cape Town, Singapore, São Paulo, Delhi

Cambridge University Press
The Edinburgh Building, Cambridge CB2 8RU, UK

www.cambridge.org
Information for this title: www.cambridge.org/9780521545402

First published 2004
7th printing 2009

Printed in the United Kingdom at the University Press, Cambridge

A catalogue record for this publication is available from the British Library

ISBN 978-0-521-54540-2 paperback

ACKNOWLEDGEMENTS
Past examination questions are reproduced by permission of
the University of Cambridge Local Examinations Syndicate.

Cover image © John Gillmoure/CORBIS

Contents

Section 3: Problem solution including algorithm design and programming concepts 37

Section 4: Software and data organisation 65

Section 5: Hardware, systems and communications 87

Section 7: Revision and examination questions 157

Preface

This book is designed to help students studying GCE O Level and IGCSE Computer Studies, and IGCSE Information Technology. It has been specifically written to cover the three syllabuses 7010 and 0420 (Computer Studies) and 0418 (Information Technology). There is an exact match between the two Computer Studies syllabuses and a broad overlap between Computer Studies and Information Technology. The book covers theory, coursework project or practical assessment, and revision and examination questions.*

IGCSE/O Level Computer Studies and IGCSE Information Technology is a modern text that has been written to encourage an active learning style by the inclusion of many tasks, questions and activities. The book is divided into seven sections. Sections 1–5 cover all the concepts and areas of knowledge needed for the written examination papers. The order of the sections follows the order of the sections of the Computer Studies syllabuses, though the material is mostly relevant to all three syllabuses. Within Sections 1,3,4 and 5, the material is generally presented in the order in which it is described in the Computer Studies syllabuses. The syllabus reference numbers in the margins indicate to Information Technology students the specific point in their syllabus that is covered by the adjacent paragraph. Although Section 2 'Systems analysis' is equally important to Computer Studies students and Information Technology students, the description given for this topic is not as detailed in the Computer Studies syllabuses as that in the Information Technology syllabus. Therefore, in Section 2 we present the material in the order in which it is described in Section 8 of the IGCSE Information Technology syllabus. Each chapter begins with a list of the learning outcomes for the chapter and ends with a summary, which gives a précis of the work contained in the chapter. Throughout these sections you will find a number of worked examples, tasks to do and example examination questions to answer. Where relevant, marks available for the example examination questions are given; we suggest possible answers for some of these questions. There is also optional extension work in many of the chapters – sometimes this provides additional information and sometimes it includes additional questions or activities.

Section 6 is devoted largely to the process of completing the coursework project for Computer Studies and to providing an opportunity to practise the IT skills needed for the practical tests in IGCSE Information Technology. Chapters 16 to 22 are written specifically for Computer Studies students and Chapter 23 is written specifically for Information Technology students. Separate lists of learning outcomes for Computer Studies students and Information Technology are given at the beginning of the section and cover the whole section.

Section 7 contains some advice about revision and examination technique, followed by examples of questions from examination papers in Chapter 24. We have supplied suggested answers for two of these papers. Chapter 25 consists of examination questions organised into topics to help with revision of specific areas.

Wherever the syllabus contents differ and the text or questions are applicable only to Computer Studies or to Information Technology, this is clearly indicated alongside the text.

Finally, at the end of the book there is a Glossary, which gives explanations of important or unusual terms that are used in the book. These terms are printed in bold type where they first appear in the text.

Examination papers

The Computer Studies courses (both O Level and IGCSE) have two examination papers.

➢ Paper 1 forms 75% of the assessment, contains mainly short-answer questions and is 2 hours 30 minutes long.

➢ Paper 2 is the coursework project and forms 25% of the assessment. The project is assessed by your school and externally moderated by CIE.

The IGCSE Information Technology course has four examination papers.

➢ Paper 1 forms 20% of the assessment, contains mainly short-answer questions and is l hour 15 minutes long The paper tests Sections 1–6 of the syllabus in the context of the applications in Section 7.1.

➢ Paper 2 forms 20% of the assessment and is similar to Paper 1, except that it tests Sections 1–6 of the syllabus in the context of the applications in Section 7.2, together with testing Section 8. It is 1 hour 15 minutes long.

➢ Paper 3 is a practical assessment, testing skills in Sections 1–5 of the syllabus and forms 30% of the assessment. It is 2 hours 45 minutes long.

➢ Paper 4 forms 30% of the assessment and is similar to Paper 3, except that it tests skills in Sections 6–8 of the syllabus. It is 2 hours 45 minutes long.

* For help with preparing for practical tests, see the following books:

Skills Award in Information Technology: Foundation Level by P.K. McBride

Skills Award in Information Technology: Standard Level by P.K. McBride

1 Applications of computers
and their social and economic implications

1 The range and scope of computer applications

Learning objectives

When you have finished this chapter you will be able to:

❖ work out the uses of different computer systems by looking at the way that they are made up;

❖ describe some of the uses of computers and be aware that there are many more;

❖ recognise some application areas from brief descriptions supplied.

1.1 Introduction

Throughout this book you will meet many examples of uses of computers. When a computer system is mentioned, try to think about what it is meant to do.

All computer systems have the following four basic parts:

➤ **input** – something that needs to be put into the computer and a way of putting it in;

➤ **processing** – work that is going to be done on what has been put in;

➤ **output** – the result of the work and a way of getting the result out;

➤ **storage** – somewhere to store things so that they are not lost when the system is switched off.

Figure 1.1 shows how these fit together.

Think in terms of these four parts whenever you come across a computer system and see if you can describe what **data** is being used (i.e. what is being put into the computer) and what the system needs in order to do what it is meant to do.

Figure 1.1
How the parts of a
computer system
fit together

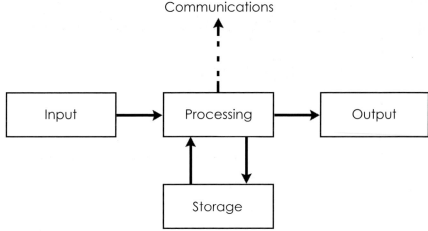

Extension work

IT4g, h

There is another part of Figure 1.1 that we have not mentioned yet – 'communications'. Most systems nowadays are able to send and receive messages to and from other computers. They may be linked in a **network**, like the one that you probably have in your school, and they may be linked to the **Internet**. When thinking about situations in which computer systems are used, try to work out what sort of communications will be needed as well.

When the school computers are connected in a network they are joined using wires but when a single computer is connected to the Internet it also needs a **modem**, which is a special piece of equipment that allows computers to link to the Internet through the telephone system.

A network in which the computers are close together is called a **local area network (LAN)**. A network in which the computers are a long way apart is called a **wide area network (WAN)**.

1.2 Types of application

IT7.2h, j

Computers used to be found only in large organisations, such as universities, where they were used for doing complicated calculations – ordinary people would never see one. Nowadays computers affect all of our lives. They range from enormously powerful machines that can forecast the weather for a week ahead to tiny **microprocessors**, which are programmed to do just one thing, such as control a washing machine. The input and the processing that take place in such microprocessors are often fairly simple and very few will communicate with other computers. Whatever the size of the computer, just think about what it is designed to do and when a question asks you to describe a system for a given purpose, remember the parts of the system listed above and try to describe them.

Extension work

IT6f

1   Make a list of devices in your home that might use a microprocessor.

Expert systems

IT7.2h, j

An **expert system** is a special type of computer system that stores all the knowledge of an expert in a particular subject so that people can ask it questions. A good example of an expert system can sometimes be found in a doctor's waiting room: patients can type their symptoms into a computer terminal and the computer will tell them whether they should wait to see the doctor. The computer contains a lot of facts about illnesses and can give advice to the patient, but if there is any doubt, the patient will be told to wait for the doctor. Although this is an expert system, compared with a human doctor the computer is actually not very expert, and it will not learn from its experience.

Some systems are cleverer than this and can learn. Think of a computer that has been programmed to play chess. It will have been given lots of facts about the game of chess and can probably play to quite a high standard. It is an expert system. But suppose the programmer forgot to put in any **information** about fool's mate, a sequence of moves that can be used to defeat a novice player very quickly. If you know those moves, you will always be able to beat the computer because it will always do the same thing in the same situation. However, if the system remembers how its opponent won and then won't let them do it again, the system has learned from its mistake. This is a much cleverer system and is said to have **artificial intelligence**.

So, an expert system knows a lot about a fairly small subject but that knowledge does not change; a system with artificial intelligence is able to learn.

Extension work

1   Identify some other expert systems and decide what data they contain that make them 'expert'.

Example question

IT7.2a

(a) List the input, processing, output and storage for each of these applications:

(i) email

(ii) weather forecasting

(iii) computer games.

(b) For each one, say what sort of communication is necessary between computers, if any.

Suggested answers

(a) (i) The input is the text that is typed into the computer using a **keyboard**.

Processing will be done in the user's computer and in the computer of the company that provides access to the Internet. Many different programs may be involved.

Output will be through the monitor screen and possibly through a **printer** if you want to print out a hard copy.

Storage may be on your computer's hard disk and on a hard drive at the firm which keeps your emails for you until you delete them.

Note: There are lots of possible answers for processing as there are many different programs that can be used with email. One you may not have thought about is spellchecking.

(ii) The input is information about weather conditions at the moment, which is probably sent automatically from a weather station to the system by things such as electronic thermometers.

Processing will involve the computer applying rules to information about the weather at the moment to work out what the weather should be like later.

Output may consist of maps to show what the weather will be like; these are probably drawn by some form of plotting machine.

Storage will be on a very large hard disk, because weather forecasting uses a lot of data.

(iii) The input will be the instructions for what the player wants to happen in the game – in a high-speed race game it might be turning a corner or overtaking another vehicle. There are a lot of input devices available for getting these instructions into the computer, such as wheels and pedals, gamepads and joysticks.

Processing will involve the computer keeping the game moving by responding to the player's input.

Output usually consists of fast-moving colour images on a screen together with sound through loudspeakers.

Storage will be on the computer's hard disk, though very little needs to be stored except for the rules of the game and perhaps your scores, as we don't normally turn the computer off halfway through a game.

(b)   (i) Computers have to communicate all over the world, so they must be linked in a WAN. The communication is going to need a modem and special measures will have to be taken to stop other people spying on the messages.

(ii) The weather stations may be a long way from the computer that does the forecast so communications will be important. Again the computers will be linked in a WAN. Communications will probably be automatic because there is no need for any people to be involved.

(iii) If there is only one player, then there does not need to be any communication. If a number of computers close together are connected so that people can play against each other, then they will probably be linked by wires in a LAN. It is also possible to play against other people over the Internet; in this case the computers will be connected in a WAN.

Summary

❖   A computer system has four basic parts:
- input
- processing
- output
- storage.

❖   Communications within and between computer systems is important.

❖   There are many different uses for computers, from controlling a washing machine to forecasting the weather.

❖   Expert systems store a lot of information about a particular topic so that they can help people perform certain tasks.

2 | The social and economic implications of the use of computers

Learning objectives

When you have finished this chapter you will be able to:

- ❖ outline some effects of computers on people and on society;
- ❖ understand the values and the dangers of using the Internet to obtain information;
- ❖ understand the pressures on businesses and organisations to computerise;
- ❖ discuss the effects of computerisation on the environment;
- ❖ state some of the implications for training of the use of computer systems;
- ❖ understand the need to protect the privacy of data;
- ❖ understand the need to ensure the security of data.

2.1 Introduction

IT6f, i, j

Your parents probably remember a time when computers were only read about in science fiction or adventure novels, where they were used by evil people who wanted to take over the world, until James Bond or some other hero came along to stop them. Computers existed in real life, but ordinary people rarely came across them and certainly did not study them in school. Your grandparents will remember a time when computers simply did not exist.

This is not really surprising. The first real electronic computer was a machine called Colossus. It was built during the Second World War to break the secret codes that the Germans used to send messages. The computer, then, is only about 60 years old. However, in that short space of time it has changed the lives of most people on the planet, it is studied in schools by most of the world's students and if computers were to suddenly disappear, life as we know it would grind to a halt because we have become so dependent upon them.

So, how do they affect us so drastically? Look at the case study for an example.

Case study: Computerisation in a steel mill

Ahmed worked in a steel mill. His was a very skilled job that took years to learn. He had to stand by the great furnaces that were full of molten metal and decide when to add the impurities, like carbon to make carbon steel, and when to pour the metal off. He knew when these things should be done because of subtle changes in the colouring of the molten metal. He had to retire when the foundry introduced computers to do his job. The computers get the timings right every time, so the finished steel is as perfect as it can be, but there are no longer any people left with the skills that Ahmed had. Soon there will be nobody left who remembers how the job can be done simply by sight. People are still employed at the foundry – someone has to press buttons on the machines and sweep the floor to keep the place tidy – but theirs are not skilled jobs like Ahmed's. This process is known as **de-skilling**, because the workers now are not as skilled as they used to be. The person who sits in the control room pressing buttons according to rules in an instruction manual is called 'semi-skilled', because it takes a bit of training but not the long apprenticeship that used to be necessary.

There are, however, some workers who have to maintain the computers and robots that now do much of the work. These are very skilled jobs, but the skills are quite different from those needed to do Ahmed's work. People who change from one type of skilled work to another are said to be **re-skilled**.

Ahmed did a very uncomfortable and dangerous job. He spent most of his working life within a few feet of molten metal. But are we any better off working with computers? There are quite a few problems associated with using computers:

➢ You don't move around very much, so you don't get as much exercise.

➢ If the chair that you are sitting in is not suitable, you are likely to get back problems.

➢ When you stare at a screen for a long time, your eyes don't move very much, which makes it difficult for the tear ducts to moisten the eyeball, leading to a condition called dry eye.

➢ When you use a computer for a long time your hands keep repeating the same actions, such as hovering over the keyboard or clicking a mouse. This can lead to repetitive strain injury (RSI), which is a bit like arthritis.

There are things which can be done to help, such as:

➢ taking regular breaks during which you get up and walk around;

➢ making sure the chair is properly designed;

➢ fitting anti-glare screens over the monitor;

➢ making sure that wires are not trailing all over the place so that people do not trip over them.

Most areas of our lives have been affected, for example:

➢ Shop assistants no longer add up the prices; they sit at computer tills that do all the work.

➢ Typists now use a **word processor** instead of a typewriter. The results are far better and the person has learned new skills so probably gets paid more. However, because they are more productive, fewer people are employed as typists in offices.

➢ Students used to do long division and learn to use log tables in maths. Now they use a calculator.

Extension work

Thinking about how computers have affected daily life is quite difficult because there are so many sides to the topic. The important thing to realise is that all instances of computer use have good and bad sides – try to recognise both. Here are some examples of the good and bad effects of computerisation on shopping:

◆ Although shop assistants no longer provide a personal service to customers, we know that the bill is always added up properly now.

◆ The old person who used to enjoy the visit to the shop is now hurried through their purchases, but everything is much cheaper because of bulk buying brought about by the ability to order through computers and keep up-to-date stock records.

◆ It is much quicker to shop nowadays and the choice is far greater than it used to be, but the stores are so big that they are built out of town on what used to be farmland.

1 Using your own experiences and those of your family and friends, make a list of ways that computers have affected your lives and how your lives would have been different if computers had not been invented.

2.2 The Internet and related topics

IT4i, k, 6f, h

One of the greatest changes has been brought about by the introduction of the Internet. The Internet is really just a big network of computers with nobody controlling it or what is placed on it. It is huge and is growing bigger every day. To find anything you need the help of a program called a **search engine**. What this does is to search incredibly quickly through the Internet to find **websites** that contain information about what you have asked for. Sometimes there seems to be too much information. I tried asking a search engine to look for 'Shakespeare' and got a list of 4,890,000 **web pages**. Unfortunately, they are not all about the playwright William Shakespeare. Many are about Shakespeare societies all over the world and then there are some that just happen to have the name Shakespeare in them, such as the Shakespeare Marine Engine Company. The problem here is not that I cannot find information, but that I find too much. I have to guess which are the best pages for the information that I want.

Another problem with information on the Internet is that nobody is in control of it. This means that anyone can create a website saying anything that they want to and they cannot be stopped. So it is possible that someone has set up a website stating that Shakespeare was Chinese, that he did not write any plays and that he was a famous aeroplane builder. All of this is nonsense, of course, but if someone who knows nothing about Shakespeare visits that website they may end up believing it. Always be very careful not to believe everything that you read on the Internet because a lot of it is not true. There are also some very nasty sites showing pornography or trying to build up hatred for others. The Internet is a wonderful tool, but it needs to be used very carefully.

Internet sites can be used to order goods and services and to pay for them using credit cards. To do this, the details on the card have to be sent to the supplier. These details are very sensitive because if they fell into the wrong hands they could be used to defraud the card holder. It is important to take great care when sending personal details across the Internet. Know who is receiving them and be certain that you can trust them. Make sure that measures are taken to stop someone else breaking into the communication and stealing your details. This last problem can be solved by making sure that your details are **encrypted** before they are sent. This means that they cannot be read by anyone who intercepts them.

IT6a

As well as credit card fraud, there is another type of theft often associated with the Internet. Next time you go on the Internet and load up a site, look at the pictures that are used and listen to any music playing. Pictures and music are often just copied from other people without asking permission or paying for the right to copy them. This is called copyright theft because the person who created the website is treating the pictures and music as their own when they actually belong to someone else. A similar thing happens a lot with software. If you borrow a game or a copy of a word processor and load it into your machine, you have broken copyright law. Lots of people do it, but that doesn't make it right.

IT4i

Many organisations have tried to overcome the problems that occur with the Internet by producing their own, small versions, which they can control. Access to them is usually limited to people who work for the organisation and have been given a **password**. There is a check that any information on site is accurate and reliable and is not going to offend anyone. These smaller, controlled, versions of the Internet are called **intranets**.

2.3 Economic reasons for computerisation

IT6f

Why do organisations use computers? Computers and the software they run are expensive to buy and need regular upgrading. Workers need training, which is not only expensive but also very time consuming, and the people who go for training on the new systems will not always be able to handle the new knowledge. Yet if we look back to the 1960s and before, we can see that businesses managed perfectly well without computer systems. So what has changed?

Think about mobile phones today. If nobody has a mobile phone, then the fact that you don't have one doesn't matter. But if your friends get them and start to communicate by phone and text messaging, then you will miss out on what is going on until you get one too. The same was true then about computers. As soon as one business got a computer system they had an advantage over their competitors. They could send out beautifully printed letters that did not have corrections on them; they had more efficient filing systems and so could answer clients' queries quickly; their secretaries and administrative people became more efficient, so they did not need so many of them, leading to a smaller wage bill and lower prices to customers. Other companies had to get computerised as well otherwise they would have lost their customers.

The use of computer systems leads to a massive investment in technology and, as we have seen, a loss of traditional skills so that the investment has to be continued. New methods are used in the steel foundry that we looked at earlier, for example:

> ➢ A computer hard disk is used to store all the data that used to be stored in a filing cabinet. This means that the company can now offer

a telephone enquiry system to its customers so that queries can be dealt with immediately and orders taken.

➤ The computer measures when to add the ingredients to the metal. Because the steel is now being produced at superb quality, it is possible to use it to produce surgical instruments for hospitals that are much sharper and stay sharper for longer.

However, there may also be some disadvantages, for example:

➤ The personal service that some customers liked has gone.

➤ The new surgical instruments may be very sharp but when they lose their edge it is no longer possible to resharpen them so they are thrown away. This puts the cost of running the operating theatre in the hospital up, so fewer operations can be done on the same budget.

The point being made here is that the introduction of computers into an established business can lead to drastic improvements, but there are also problems that can occur.

Extension work

IT7.2k

Scenario: Computerisation in a local store

In a small town there are two stores that sell food, general produce and household articles. Customers ask the assistant who greets them for the goods that they want and the assistant collects the goods from shelves behind the counter and keeps a total of the amount owed by the customer.

This system has worked perfectly well in the two stores for many years. Then one of the stores decides to introduce a computerised system into the store. The system will power **point-of-sale terminals** and use the **barcodes** on the goods to find out what they are. The system will also be used for maintaining the stock records and automatically ordering goods when necessary.

In small groups, or as a class, discuss the following questions:

1 What are the things that the shopper will notice when they go to the store with the new system?

2 Will all the shoppers from both stores be drawn to the modern computerised one, or can you see reasons why some will still want to shop in the old-fashioned store?

3 What will be the effect on the workers in the store? Don't forget to include *all* the people who work in the store.

4   What will be the effect on the stock that is available for the customers to buy?

5   Why does the store with the new system have fewer specially discounted stock items because they are out of date?

6   Why does the store with the new system have more special offers available?

Scenario: Computerisation in a local store (continued)

The store with the new system decides to offer a new service whereby customers who are too busy to come to get their own shopping or who are disabled can email an order to the store over the Internet. The store will then arrange to have the order delivered.

7   How can the store make sure that the goods are paid for?

8   What are the disadvantages to the customer?

9   Is this very different from the old system that allowed customers to telephone in their orders? Is the system coming round full circle?

2.4 Changes to the environment and training practices

IT6e, f, i

When computers were first brought into offices, people thought that there would be a massive reduction in the amount of paper used. Communications would be mainly done electronically and there would be no need to retype letters because they would be printed perfectly first time. The truth has been quite the opposite. Whereas in the past any mistakes were corrected on the original typing, nowadays when a simple mistake is spotted, it is corrected and the document is printed again. When someone arranges a meeting in an office, they will print a memo to send to each person rather than putting a notice on a notice board. Even if individuals are sent an electronic memo, they will probably still print it out on their own printers. A lot more paper is wasted today than used to be, which is having a distinct environmental effect. On the other hand, offices are now much quieter, without the noise of all those typewriters. Some people have a computer terminal at home that is linked to their head office. This means they can work at home, which can be wonderful because they no longer have to drive into work and can spend more time with their families. The number of cars on the roads is reduced so there are fewer harmful gases from the exhausts and those cars that are on the road are working more efficiently because they too have computers in their engines. However, many people do not like working from home because they miss mixing with their fellow workers and begin to feel isolated.

People who rely on computer systems for their work need to be trained properly. Training used to involve a specialist trainer taking a class or a small group of people and leading them through the types of task that they may be expected to do. The specialist would have to be paid and workers would need time off to do the training; it might even be necessary to shut the organisation for a short time. This was all very expensive, so what often happens nowadays is that the training course is a specially written computer program, probably in the form of a **multimedia package** (a program using a number of different elements, such as text, graphics, animation and sound – see Chapter 11), which the worker can do at their own pace and in their own time. They may even be encouraged to take it home and do it there.

Extension work

IT7.2e

Schools are following businesses in relying more and more heavily on computers. They are used to teach not only IT and computing, but all the other subjects on the curriculum as well. This type of training or learning is known as **computer-aided learning (CAL)**.

In small groups, answer the following questions:

1   How far can this use of computers sensibly be taken in a school?

2   What restrictions are there in a school that there would not be in a business?

3   How have the people in the school been affected so far and how would they be affected in the future if there were to be even more reliance on computers in schools?

2.5 Issues of privacy and access to data

IT4j

As computers have become widely used, protecting the **privacy of data** has become very important. Most computer applications, other than simple computer games, store data that can be used in the program. One of the great benefits of using computers is that the stored data is easily accessible, and because computers make communications very easy the data stored on one computer can be transmitted to another one. If the data consists of the prices a supermarket is charging for its food, then it really doesn't matter very much if someone looks at the data who perhaps shouldn't. However, if the data contained the prices a supermarket was going to charge in the future, they would not be very happy if another supermarket managed to see this, because the competitor could then set their own prices accordingly. If the data contains someone's personal details, it is even more important to limit access to it. In fact, most data contains something that someone would like to keep private, sometimes for a reason that is not obvious. The lack of data protection was becoming very serious back in the early 1980s, when even bank accounts were unprotected so that they were easy to look at, and many other pieces of information were at risk. Governments around the world began to introduce legislation to protect the data from people who should not see it and also tried to make sure the data was accurate. Each of the laws passed was slightly different because they were in different countries, but most included measures to cover the following things:

➢ Data stored on computers must be protected from access by people who do not have a need to see it. This is normally done by issuing passwords to people who are allowed access to the data.

➢ Data that contains information about an individual cannot be passed from one organisation to another if that person does not want this to happen.

➢ Data must be accurate and up to date.

➢ Data must be collected fairly and only used for the original purpose.

➢ A person has a right to see any data that contains information about them, and to ask for it to be changed if necessary.

➢ When the data is no longer needed, it must be destroyed.

The obvious way to protect the data from people who should not see it is to use passwords, as mentioned above. These can be arranged in what is known as a hierarchy. This means that different people are given different rights to see the data. Imagine a doctors' surgery – lots of very sensitive data will be stored about each of the patients. The receptionist needs to have access to patients' addresses and phone numbers so that letters can be sent out and patients can be rung up to change appointment times and so on, but they should not be able to see patients' medical records. Individual doctors only need to see the medical histories for their own patients. The head of the surgery needs to see all the patient records in order to keep a check on the doctors. There are other people who work there and each will need to see different things. Each person will have a password that allows them to see different sets of the data; the more important people in the organisation will have more powerful passwords that allow them to see more of the data.

Extension work

Another point to consider is that if a lot of people have access to the data, then there are more people in a position to change it. This can lead to problems. For example, if a set of data in a supermarket has beans priced at 1 dollar and someone changes this to 2 dollars when they should not have, then shoppers will pay the wrong price. Worse would be if one of the checkouts was using a list of prices that had been changed and the others were not. This time the customers would be charged different amounts depending on which checkout they used. This would be a disaster for the shop if the customers found out, because people would stop trusting them. This reliance that we have on data and the fact that we tend to assume that what computers tell us is correct means that the data needs to be accurate – we say that the data must have **integrity**. In other words it must be reliable.

1   A lot of data about students is stored on a college computer system. Make a list of the different data that would be stored. Divide the different data into groups that need to be seen by different people and hence devise a hierarchy of people on the college staff with rights to the different data groups.

2.6 Security of data

IT6b, c, d

These days the **security of data** (i.e. making sure it is not lost or destroyed) is just as important as protecting the privacy of data. The most dangerous threat to data is that the system may fail in some way causing it to be lost. This can be catastrophic. The supermarket that is relying on the computerised checkouts would have to shut if it lost its data because the goods do not have the prices on them, just a barcode. The computer checkout would still try to read the barcode, but it would find no data about the prices, so the assistants would not be able to sell anything. Sometimes a failure that wipes out **files** would just be annoying – imagine how you would feel if your teacher told you at the start of a lesson that your project work had been lost and that you had to start it again! But sometimes it can be far worse. If a bank lost all its files, it would go out of business because it wouldn't know who owed it money or who it owed money to. There are different levels of importance of files, but even if only your project were lost and nobody else's, it would still be important to you.

The simplest way to overcome the problem of lost data is not to rely on just one copy of the files. A second copy, called a **back-up file**, is normally made. The back-up file is very rarely used because it is very rare for something to go wrong, but if it does go wrong, the back-up is there so that we have not lost all the data. You do not have to start your project again, the bank does not have to close. Your project is probably on a back-up file that your teacher makes once a week. This is not perfect because you could still lose a whole week's work, but the rest would be saved. Losing a week of transactions would still be a disaster for a bank, though, so bank files are probably backed-up every half an hour or so. Your teacher won't bother with more than one back-up file because the chance of both the original and the back-up being destroyed is so small it is not worth bothering with, but the bank will probably have four or five back-up files, just in case.

Another way that the files can be destroyed is by fire. If the back-up file is in the same room as the computer, then a fire would burn the back-up file as well, so it needs to be kept safe somewhere away from the main computer.

Extension work

So far we have only talked about accidents happening to the files, but sometimes the damage is deliberate. Some people get pleasure from trying to break into other people's computer systems and doing them serious damage. There are two ways that this is done. The first is called **hacking** and actually involves someone taking control of your computer and its files. This is normally done when the system is connected to the Internet. The hacker tries to break the passwords to get onto the system, and if successful will read files and steal information or try to destroy the systems. Computers need to be protected from these attacks. One way is to use passwords, but another is to allow access to a system only through a computer that is not used for anything else; this is called a **firewall** and should stop anyone who is not authorised gaining access. Another method is to make the computer system produce a log of all attempts to gain access. In this way any unauthorised access can be picked up and traced back to where it came from. Finally, if all else fails, it is possible to stop the hacker from reading the files by using a secret code. This is called encryption and the files are said to have been encrypted.

Another method of attacking a system is to use a computer **virus**. A virus is a small program that tries to make copies of itself and to get itself transmitted from one computer system to another. If it is not spotted, it may make so many copies that it wipes out the computer's storage because there ends up being no room for anything else. Fortunately, there are many **virus protection** programs on the market. They are stored in the computer and spend all their time looking for programs that look like viruses. When they find one, they either tell you about it or just erase it. There are a lot of viruses around, particularly on the Internet, which makes it very important to be careful when you download something from the net.

Task

Most schools have two types of computer system: one that is used by students and teachers for such things as project work and one that is used for school administration. As a group, quiz your teacher about the system with the student projects on it to get answers to the following questions:

1   What files are stored and how are they arranged?

2   What password measures are used to stop people looking at things they shouldn't see?

3   What sort of back-ups are done, how often and where are they kept?

4   What protection does the system have from viruses?

Ask your school administrator if they will come along and talk with the class about the school administration system. Ask the same sorts of question as you asked your teacher and see what differences there are between the two systems.

Summary

- ❖ People's lives have been changed for ever by computers in the areas of work, leisure, the environment, home and school.

- ❖ All change has a good side and a bad side.

- ❖ Training in the workplace and in schools and colleges has been changed by the use of computers.

- ❖ Most data is sensitive in some way, so access to data needs to be controlled, for example by using passwords, and to be protected from people who try to break into computer communications, for example by encryption.

- ❖ Because we rely so much on data in computer systems it needs to be protected against loss, for example by making back-up copies, and it needs to be accurate.

2 Systems analysis

The layout of this section follows the layout of Section 8 of the IGCSE Information Technology syllabus, but the work is equally relevant to Computer Studies. It is important you study this section before embarking on Section 3.

When an organisation feels one of its systems has problems or is in need of improvement, a **systems analyst** studies the system to determine where the problems are and how the system can be improved. The analyst then plans the implementation of the solution and hands the plans on to a software team to produce the solution. The analyst then plans how the system is going to be imported into the organisation and arranges for continuing maintenance of the system. This whole process is known as **systems analysis** and the stages can be summarised as:

> ➢ analysis
> ➢ **design**
> ➢ implementation
> ➢ documentation
> ➢ evaluation/maintenance.

Don't worry too much about these stages, or the items within the stages – they are different in every textbook you look at. The stages in this book are simply copies of those in the IGCSE Information Technology syllabus.

One very important thing to remember as we go through this work is that when a problem is solved in this way, we shouldn't think of the stages as being in a straight line. The analyst does not start at the beginning and work straight through to the end. They will perhaps reach one stage and realise that they need to go back and find out something else. Or they may discover that something does not work properly, so they go back and change the design. This process is often described as a waterfall or cascade (as illustrated in the figure below). At each level it is possible to go back to a previous stage.

The process of systems analysis

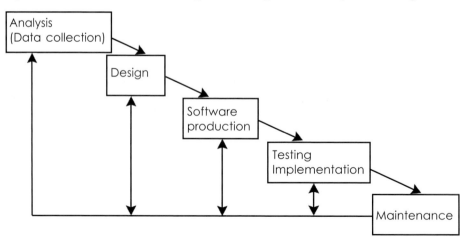

3 Analysis

Learning objectives

When you have finished this chapter you will be able to:

- ❖ state the importance of identifying the problem correctly and describe the place of the systems analyst within the system;

- ❖ outline the advantages and disadvantages of four methods of data collection;

- ❖ understand the need to analyse and record the data collected.

3.1 Introduction

The very first part of the analysis stage consists of problem definition and a feasibility study. Problem definition is the most important part of the whole process, because if the analyst does not understand what the problem is, then any solution they propose may solve the wrong problem.

Problem definition always involves a compromise between the people in the organisation and the systems analyst. The people in the organisation know how their business works, what the nature of the problem is and how much they can spend. The analyst knows about computers and what is possible. First the analyst is told what is wanted. He or she produces a report that states what is possible. This is called the feasibility study. At this stage the proposals are still very sketchy, but if the feasibility study is accepted, then the analyst needs to find out as much as possible about the organisation and the problem to be solved. This leads to the collection of information.

3.2 Collection of information

This collection of information can be done in a number of ways:

➤ Observation – The systems analyst can learn a massive amount from simply watching what is going on in the area of the organisation with the problem. It is very useful because no planning is necessary and it does not involve working with other people, but the disadvantage is that people tend not to behave in a normal way if they know they are being watched. Point a camera at someone and you will understand what I mean.

➤ Interviews – If the systems analyst wants to find out what is going on and, particularly, what is not working properly in an organisation, the obvious thing to do is to ask the people who work there, and those who operate the system at the moment. This is the best way of finding things out because the questions do not have to be fixed in advance; the analyst can change them according to the answers the interviewees give. The disadvantage is that interviewing takes a lot of time.

➤ Questionnaires – These are much less time-consuming than interviews because every worker can fill one in at the same time. The disadvantage is that they may not be taken seriously and, unlike the interview, the analyst cannot change questions halfway through.

➤ Document collection – A lot can be discovered about an organisation by examining the documents that it uses. The analyst will be looking for answers to questions such as: How is the data collected? What data is collected? What happens to this data after it has been collected? A disadvantage is that the documentation is often difficult to understand, so it may be necessary to ask someone to explain it. This means we are back to the interview again.

3.3 Requirements specification

While the analyst is collecting data about the problem, a list will be forming of things that will be necessary in any solution of the problem. This list is the **requirements specification** and will include some details about the storage requirements and what the organisation wants the system to do. It may also contain information about the desired **hardware** and **software**. Think of this as being a 'wish list' of what the organisation would like (it will be altered later) as well as being the specified minimum requirements that the system must meet.

3.4 Recording data

The data-collection methods outlined above will provide a large amount of data about the present system and about the flow of information through the system. This raw data needs to be collated and studied, so that it can be turned into useful information and recorded in some way. Sometimes this will bring to light areas where there are gaps in the data collected. For example, the analyst may realise that important questions weren't asked in the interviews, so further interviews may be needed.

The best way to deal with information like this is probably to record it in a diagram that shows the passage of the data around the system and what is done to that data. This sort of diagram is called a data flow diagram or flowchart and you will find out more about these, and other diagrams, in Section 3.

Summary

❖ The systems analyst and the owner of the problem need to compromise over a possible solution.

❖ The systems analyst needs to collect information about the present situation using observation, interviews, questionnaires and document collection.

❖ A requirements specification is drawn up, which will then be refined in the light of experience in the following stages.

❖ All the data collected must be collated and recorded in some way. Diagrams can be useful.

4 Design

4.1 Output designs

All computer systems consist of:

➢ input

➢ processing

➢ output

➢ storage

as described in Chapter 1. The purpose of the design stage is to decide what the output should look like. It may seem odd to start from what appears to be 'the wrong end', but the analyst's job is to produce a system that will do a particular thing. In other words, the really important part is to decide what the organisation wants to happen in the end. If the analyst can get the end product to their liking, they are likely to accept the whole solution. Imagine the organisation is a mail order company and the analyst has been asked to produce a system that will allow the telephone receptionists to take orders over the phone. The company bosses are only concerned with whether the people on the phones can search to see if stock is available and then place an order. They are not really interested in how the system does it. The analyst will design what the output screens will look like and then produce what is known as a **prototype**. It won't work yet because no processing has been designed, after all there is no data yet! This prototype is good enough, though, for the management and the workers who will actually use it to be able to tell whether it will be able to do all the things that they want it to do.

4.2 Input designs

The next stage is to design input screens that will produce all the data the system needs in order to create the information that users want on their output screens and in their reports. These input screens go through the same prototyping process as the output screens. Once the decisions have been taken about the data that is required, the analyst has to decide how that data can be collected and what sort of data input should be used. For instance:

➢ Will automatic data collection be used? For example, a sensor telling the system when someone enters a building, or what the temperature of a process is.

➢ Are questionnaires (**data-capture forms**) going to be used? If they are, should they be designed so that the answer sheets can be read by a special mark-reading machine?

➢ Is the data going to be input by someone using a keyboard and screen?

There are many different ways to input data, so the analyst has to choose one and then design a way of capturing data that can be used with it.

Many people think that you should use a pencil and paper for design work, but when you think of all the different design aids and things like **wizards** that are available on the computer, it makes sense to do the design straight onto the screen.

4.3 Data storage

Now that the analyst knows what the input is going to be and what the output should be, it is possible to design the data storage. Among the questions that need to be considered are:

➢ How much data needs to be stored?

➢ Will the amount of data that needs to be stored increase in the future, as the needs of the organisation change? By how much?

➢ How often are the different data items going to be accessed?

> ➤   Who should have access to the data and how will that access be controlled?

> ➤   What sort of hardware is going to be needed for the storage?

When data is input to the system, it will have to be checked to make sure that it is accurate. Special routines called **validation** routines are set up to do this; we will be returning to this in Section 4.

Summary

- ❖   It is important that the analyst understands what the end user wants from the system.

- ❖   Prototype designs of the output are produced first. These lead to the production of designs for the system's input and storage.

- ❖   Data entered into the system must be as accurate as possible.

---

5 | Implementation

Learning objectives

When you have finished this chapter you will be able to:

❖   state why it is important to have a test strategy and a test plan;

❖   explain why different test data is needed for different situations;

❖   distinguish between real data and test data;

❖   understand the need to train the people who will be using the solution and the need to produce the data files;

❖   describe the sort of planning needed in advance of implementing the solution into the business;

❖   outline three different implementation methods.

5.1 Processing

After the input, storage and output have been designed, the obvious next stage would seem to be to produce the software. However, there is another stage that must come first.

When the software has been produced, it will be necessary to test it to make sure that it does what it is supposed to. The danger of leaving the testing until after the software has been produced is that there is a tendency to make the tests fit the software rather than the other way around. Obviously it is not possible to test something that does not exist, but it is important to decide how the software is going to be tested when it has been produced. To do this a **test strategy** is needed. This involves:

➢   deciding which parts of the software functions need to be tested;

➢   drawing up a **test plan** that includes what tests will be done and what data will be used in the tests.

The test strategy will normally include testing all the different parts of the software that a user can use and making sure that the results are what are expected. Both test data and real data should be used. Test data is data that is invented to make sure that the system can be thoroughly tested. It includes some data that could be part of the solution, some that would be right on the edge of being acceptable and some that should produce error messages. Real data is used because this will be typical of the data that the system will need to handle from day to day; the analyst needs to make sure it doesn't produce any unexpected results.

One thing to remember is that you cannot test whether a piece of software will always work. Imagine a simple program that adds two numbers together. A sensible test to see if it works would be to input the numbers 3 and 4. If the software gives the answer 7, it has passed that test. But what about 5 and 9, or 7 and 3.5? An infinite number of tests would have to be done to prove that the software always works, which of course is impossible. A better approach is to think of tests that would prove that the software does not work. When these tests fail, you can assume that the software works.

5.2 Implementing the solution into the organisation

When the system has been produced and thoroughly tested, it then has to be implemented into the organisation for which it has been designed. How this is done will be decided beforehand because there are some choices to be made and a lot of work to be done.

If a completely new system has been designed, doing something that was not done before, then there is no choice: the system has to be put in place and switched on. However, most systems are designed to take over a task from an older system, so a **changeover** from one system to another is involved. The first thing to be done is to buy and install new hardware. It is possible that all the old hardware will be good enough, but this is unlikely. If only some of the equipment needs replacing, then staff may be able to carry on working. However, it is quite likely that the business will need to shut down. For example, if all the checkouts in a supermarket are being replaced, the store will probably have to close while it is being done.

After the hardware has been installed, the files of data have to be loaded onto the system. If they already exist in electronic form, this may be easy, but if the old system was paper-based, then all the data has to be typed in.

Finally, the staff have to be trained to use the new system. If they are used to a computerised system already, then the training may not need to be very extensive. However, if they are not used to a computerised system, the training has to be carefully planned. It is possible that even with training some of the workers may not be able to learn how to use the new system; this causes a major social problem.

The implementation of a new system can be carried out in a number of ways. There are three different changeover methods that you need to know about:

➤ Direct changeover – This is the simplest method. Imagine a new checkout system for a supermarket. If the implementation is to be done by direct changeover, the supermarket will shut one night, all the old checkouts will be ripped out, the new system will be put in and the supermarket will reopen. Although this is a simple method, it takes a lot of planning. All the files have to be ready to load, all the workers need to have been trained in advance and the system must have been properly tested. If the checkouts don't work when they are switched on, the store will have to close because they cannot go back to the old system. This was how the UK stock market was computerised in the 1980s. The old market closed on Friday night and the computers were all switched on the following Monday morning. Unfortunately, there was an error in the software, which made all the computers sell shares and carry on selling them. By the time human beings had intervened to stop the computers, half the value of companies had been wiped off the stock market and many people had been ruined.

➤ Phased implementation – Think about the supermarket again and imagine that only the fresh vegetable section is changed over to the new system while all the rest carries on with the old. If the new system doesn't work, it won't matter too much because only a small part of the supermarket has been computerised. If it does work, staff can take turns working on the fresh vegetables counters to get some practice using the new system. After the vegetables section is working perfectly, fresh meats might be next, and so on. Eventually all the parts of the supermarket system would have been phased in and the whole thing would be running. This takes a long time and there are two systems working until the changeover is completed. However, the supermarket is never in danger of having to shut and the staff are all able to get plenty of training, so it is a much friendlier method.

➤ Parallel running – This implementation method involves old and new systems working at the same time. In the supermarket this would mean customers going through the old tills with their shopping and then immediately going through the new checkouts, where all their shopping would be added up again! This would test the new system properly because it would be possible to check the second bill against the first for every transaction – any difference and something has gone wrong. Of course, this would be a crazy way of implementation in a supermarket because it would be extremely expensive and the customers would go to the shop down the road. However, when the examination board changed the computer system that works out your exam grades and prints the certificates, they used parallel running to make sure everything was all right, because it would have been disastrous for the candidates if the new system printed the wrong grades.

Summary

❖ A test strategy needs to be devised to determine how the testing is to be carried out and a test plan is needed to show how this strategy is to be achieved.

❖ Test data is data chosen to test a particular aspect of the software solution, it may never occur in real life, while the real data is typical data that the software will cope with when in operation.

❖ Three common methods of implementing new systems are direct changeover, phased implementation and parallel running.

6 Documentation

Learning objectives

When you have finished this chapter you will be able to:

❖ describe two types of documentation associated with problem solving and be able to distinguish between them;

❖ outline the typical contents of technical documentation and state the reasons why the items of documentation are necessary;

❖ outline the typical contents of user documentation and state the reasons why the items of documentation are necessary.

6.1 Introduction

Sometimes a small simple problem can be solved by a single person who uses the system. In this situation it would not be necessary to do much advance planning or to write detailed notes about the solution. However, most problems aren't like this. For anything bigger, full notes have to be kept about how the problem was solved, and instructions on how to use the new system need to be written. These are usually produced as two separate sets of documents, known as **technical documentation** and **user documentation**. These are described in more detail below.

One important thing to remember about the documentation is that it is not just tacked on at the end of the solution. The documentation should be produced while the solution is being developed. This is especially important for the technical documentation because there will almost certainly be more than one person producing the solution and each person involved needs to know what everyone else is doing.

6.2 Technical documentation

The technical documentation is the information about the solution that a technician, or someone who has to update the system in the future, needs in order to understand how the system works. It will include:

➢ details of any programming that was done, such as the original **algorithms** (which might be in the form of **pseudocode** or programming diagrams – see Section 3) and the code that has been fully annotated with explanations of what each instruction does;

➢ **system flowcharts**, which are diagrams showing how the hardware fits together and where all the data is stored and processed;

➢ the hardware requirements of the system, including sizes of all the files and the capabilities of the processor;

➢ the software requirements, which may be details of software that has been bought in and changed to match the solution or of software that has been written especially for this problem solution;

➢ information about file structures, in other words what type of data is in each file (not 'Ahmed Iqbal is in class 3D for computing in room 6', but a statement to say that the file holds student names, the class they are in, the subject they are doing and the room it is taught in); this is needed so that the file structures can be altered in the future;

➢ details of the **variables** that have been used so that if a change is made to the code and a new variable is used, it does not clash with one that has already been used;

➢ details of validation routines (see Section 4).

6.3 User documentation

The other part of the documentation is that provided for the people who are actually going to use the system. The person who is sitting at a computer terminal and answering customer queries by using a **database** does not need to know how the database finds things or in what form data about the price of the goods is stored. They just need to know how to look up the price. The user documentation tells them how to do it. It tells them other things as well, such as:

➢ what sort of hardware and software is used, though in much less detail than in the technical documentation;

➢ what sort of input is needed and how to input it;

➢   what sort of output is produced and what it should look like;

➢   some samples of successful operations showing what to expect;

➢   the meanings of any error messages that might appear on the screen;

➢   what to do when something goes wrong.

Summary

❖   It is important to keep full documentation about solutions to all but the simplest problems.

❖   There are two types of documentation associated with creating or modifying a system to solve a problem: technical documentation and user documentation.

❖   Technical documentation is for the group of people who understand (or need to understand) how the solution works.

❖   User documentation is for the group of people who don't care how the system works but simply want to be able to use it.

7 Evaluation/maintenance

> ## Learning objectives
>
> When you have finished this chapter you will be able to:
>
> ❖ state how the success of a solution is measured;
>
> ❖ describe problem solving as a circular process, rather than as a linear one;
>
> ❖ explain why the finished software needs to be tested by different users.

7.1 Evaluation against objectives

Before the solution was ever produced in software form, the systems analyst and the organisation for whom the system was being developed agreed a set of things that the finished solution must do. These are called the **objectives of a solution**. This is extremely important because when the solution is completed it will be measured against these objectives. If it does not satisfy the objectives, the problem will not have been solved (and the analyst will not get paid). The problem solution will be considered a success if the objectives are met.

7.2 Limitations and necessary improvements

It is important that the people involved with the solution accept the fact that it is always going to be possible to find other things that need doing and things that could be done in a slightly better way. They should realise that the production of the work is not the end of the process but that continual improvement can be made. In other words, the process is circular rather than linear. This is the reason for all that technical documentation – so that someone can come along and change things later when necessary.

7.3 Testing

The solution will have been tested by the people who produced it. However, these people tend to be those who know about computers and know what the software was meant to do. When the system has been installed and is being used by the ordinary workers in the organisation, they will find problems with it that the computer-literate testers simply did not think of. As these problems arise it is going to be important to have technicians around who can repair the system – another reason for that technical documentation.

Summary

❖　Systems analysis is a circular process, which implies that the system will need regular maintenance after the software is completed.

❖　Different types of people will tend to find different errors in the software when they are testing it because of their different expectations.

3 Problem solution

including algorithm design and programming concepts

In this section you will learn the stages necessary to design, develop and implement the solution to a problem.

Information Technology students need to be able to identify the components of the technical documentation, such as program coding, system flowcharts, program flowcharts, as well as the components of the user documentation. Information Technology students need to study Chapter 8 only and can ignore any reference to top-down design.

Computer Studies students will need to study the whole section, including the extension work at the end of Chapter 10.

8 Methods relating to the solution of a problem

Learning objective

When you have finished this chapter you will be able to:

❖ break down a problem into smaller stages.

8.1 Devise a strategy

Whenever there is a problem to solve, whether or not we use a computer to assist with the solution, we need to establish a strategy that we can apply. This strategy consists of several stages and is closely linked with systems analysis, which was covered in Section 2. The three main stages are:

➢ understand the problem

➢ devise a solution

➢ test the solution.

However, we need to develop an extra stage:

➢ document the solution

so that the solution can be maintained and/or developed in the future. To demonstrate this process we are going to look at a particular problem, namely: 'Read in a date and convert it into the number of days since the start of the calendar year'.

8.2 Understand the problem

At first the problem appears to be quite simple, but when we consider it in more detail it becomes more complicated. For example, at the input stage we need to consider the format of the input date. It could be any of the following: 1 July 2003; 1st July 2003; July 1st 2003; 1 July 03; 1/7/03; 7/1/03; 030701. Other variations are also possible. And what happens if the current year is a leap year? The solution will need to take that into account.

8.3 Devise a solution

Any problem can be solved using the input–process–output model. The solution to our problem can be broken down into three stages:

1   input the date;

2   calculate the number of days since 1 January;

3   output the result.

However, stages 1 and 2 can be divided into smaller tasks. Stage 1 will need to accept only correctly formatted dates and reject any incorrect dates. The user could be prompted to input the date in a specific format or the user could input the date in any format and the solution would recognise any valid format. Obviously the second option will be much more difficult to achieve since there is a large number of valid formats for a date. Stage 2 could make use of iterative techniques to calculate the correct number of days. **Iteration** is a process of repeating a sequence of steps until the required answer has been achieved. In this case, one way to solve the problem would be to add one day to the last date (the first time we do this the last date is 1 January) and compare it with the date that was input. If the two dates match, then we have calculated the required number of days. If the dates do not match, then we repeat the process of adding one day to the last date and compare this with the date that was input. We continue to do the same process until the two dates match.

8.4 Test the solution

Once we have devised what we think is a working solution, then we need to test it using data for which we know the answer. In the given example, the answer for 1 July 2003 should be 181. If the date was 1 July 2004, then the answer should be 182. We need to test the solution with three types of data:

➢   normal

➢   abnormal

➢   extreme.

These types of data are discusssed in more detail on page 145.

8.5 Document the solution

We need to document the solution to help anyone who will be using the system and anyone who needs to revise the solution in the future. Documentation should therefore consist of two separate types:

➢   user documentation

➢   technical documentation.

User documentation

This is sometimes known as the user guide or user manual. This guide should include:

➢ an overview of what the solution does;

➢ information about how to install the solution;

➢ some examples of how certain functions work;

➢ what to do when certain errors occur;

➢ sample screen displays and/or output.

Technical documentation

Technical documentation should provide a programmer or systems analyst with an explanation of how the system works and include notes to assist in any future amendments. It should contain details of both the system and the software. Systems documentation describes:

➢ the systems analysis – what is expected of the system;

➢ the overall design;

➢ the test plan and test data together with the expected results.

Software documentation consists of information about:

➢ the purpose of the software;

➢ any restrictions or limitations on the use of the software;

➢ the format for input data;

➢ the format for printed output;

➢ **top-down design** – the breaking down of a large problem into smaller subproblems or **modules**;

➢ program listing – a complete list of the instructions contained in the computer program that has been written;

➢ **data tables** – a list of the variables used in the computer program;

➢ **data dictionaries** – a list that stores details of the data items in a database; it should include details of field names and the tables where they are held, the field types and lengths, and any specific format or validation technique.

If we put together all of these elements, we can see that the solution to any problem can be devised by the following process:

➢ understand the problem;

➢ devise a solution;

    ◆ input

    ◆ process

    ◆ output;

➢ test the solution;

➢ document the solution.

Worked example

Problem

Read in ten numbers and display their total.

Understanding the problem

Ten numbers will be entered and only the total is to be output.

Solution

Top-down design is simply three modules, components or stages, as shown in Figure 8.1.

Figure 8.1
Top-down design

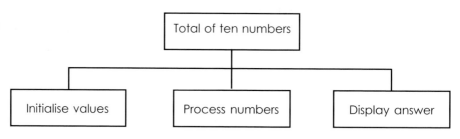

The second stage of processing the numbers could make use of a loop repeated ten times, so we need to count the number of values we are adding. We can use a variable TOTAL to store the cumulative total of the numbers and we can use a variable COUNT to count the number of numbers. We can now break down our problem into smaller tasks (see Figure 8.2).

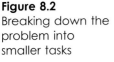

Figure 8.2
Breaking down the
problem into
smaller tasks

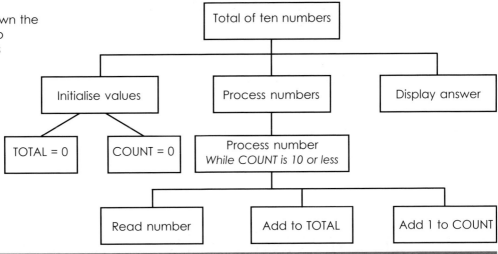

Tasks

Write down the stages of solving the following problems.

Problem 1

Read a list of numbers that represent the cost of buying some items. The end of the list is to be indicated by using a cost of 0. Display the total cost of the items and the number of items purchased.

Problem 2

Read a list of numbers that represent money being paid into your bank account (positive numbers) or money being taken out of the account (minus numbers). The end of the list is to be indicated by a value of your choice. Display the total money paid in and the total of the money taken out of your account.

Summary

❖ All solutions to any problem can be represented by the single generic process:

◆ understand the problem

◆ devise a solution
   – input
   – process
   – output

◆ test

◆ document.

9 Algorithms and their methods of representation

> **Learning objectives**
>
> When you have finished this chapter you will be able to:
>
> ❖   use a variety of pseudocode structures;
>
> ❖   design and test a suitable algorithm to solve a problem;
>
> ❖   distinguish between high-level and low-level programming languages.

9.1 What is pseudocode?

Pseudocode is a method of describing the design of a system. It uses words similar to those found in programming languages but not the actual strict rules of structure and syntax. It most frequently resembles a mixture of English and a programming language. As an example, the following is a typical pseudocode solution to the problem of sorting names into alphabetical order.

```
Enter names
Repeat
    Set check to 'No'
    Look at the first pair of names
    Repeat
        While names out of order do
        Begin
            Swap names
        Set check to 'Yes'
        End
        Look at the next pair of names
    Until no more pairs of names
Until check is 'No'
Output names in order
```

9.2 What is an algorithm?

An algorithm is simply a sequence of instructions written to solve a given problem. It may be devised to describe the operation of a complete system or it may relate to one particular part of that system, so that the complete solution to a problem can be described by a series of separate algorithms. In this chapter we shall look at some techniques that help to describe algorithms by the use of diagrams and pseudocode. We shall also suggest an algorithm that can be used to write algorithms.

One of the simplest ways to display the solution to a problem is by using a flowchart. Flowcharts can be used to illustrate systems and programs. Each type of task in the system or program being illustrated is represented by a symbol. Figure 9.1 shows the basic shapes used in program flowcharts, which were originally used to describe in detail the different sections of computer programs.

Figure 9.1
Program flowchart symbols

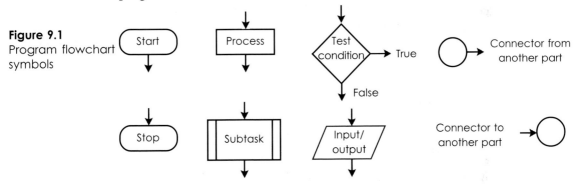

Consider the simple problem of converting a distance given in metres into centimetres. The solution is to take the distance in metres and multiply by 100. We could represent this in the form of a flowchart, as shown in Figure 9.2.

Figure 9.2
A simple flowchart

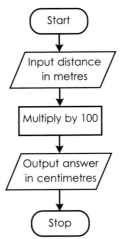

All problems can be solved by the use of the input–process–output method. As a first step in the formulation of any algorithm you should determine what data is to be input and what processing needs to be done on the data to get the required output.

Tasks

Problem 1

Draw a flowchart to add together two numbers.

Problem 2

A microprocessor is used to control the air-conditioning unit of a house.

1   What temperatures are needed for the microprocessor to operate the system?

2   What processing of the temperatures takes place?

3   What action does the microprocessor take in response to the data processing?

4   Complete the program flowchart shown in Figure 9.3, which can be used to control the air conditioning.

Figure 9.3
A program flowchart to control air conditioning

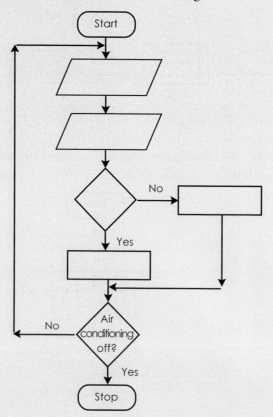

Such flowcharts serve a limited purpose, since they can become complicated and show far too much detail when dealing with large, complex problems. There are often many interconnected links and the chart may extend over several pages, making it difficult to see the overall solution. A further development is the use of system flowcharts to describe how the system works. Figure 9.4 shows a selection of symbols used in system flowcharts.

Figure 9.4
System flowchart symbols

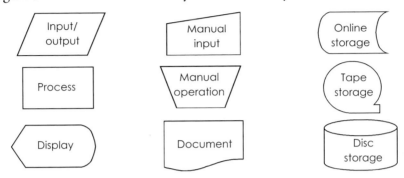

There is a technique to drawing system flowcharts. Unlike program flowcharts there are no start, stop or decision boxes, and the arrows show the flow of data within the system and not the order of operation. System flowcharts are easier to read if the data-capture processes are situated on the left, processes down the middle and storage and/or output on the right.

Worked example

Problem

Consider the example of a pupil database within a school and how to create a system flowchart to represent the information provided.

Table 9.1
Input–process–output model for a pupil database

Data is collected by the office staff, keyed into the system and validated. Any errors are displayed and the acceptable data is stored on disk and merged with the existing pupil database. During the year, changes to the data are collected by teachers and keyed in by the office staff, and the master file is updated. At any time the database can be searched to find data on individual pupils. This is summarised in Table 9.1.

Input data	Processing	Storage	Output
Pupil data collected from pupils	Data validated	Stored to new pupils database	Errors displayed
Changes to pupil data	Data validated Update to database	Stored to database master file	Errors displayed
Request for specific information on a pupil	Search for individual pupil details		Details displayed

Solution

This can be represented in the following system flowchart (Figure 9.5).

Figure 9.5
Pupil database
system flowchart

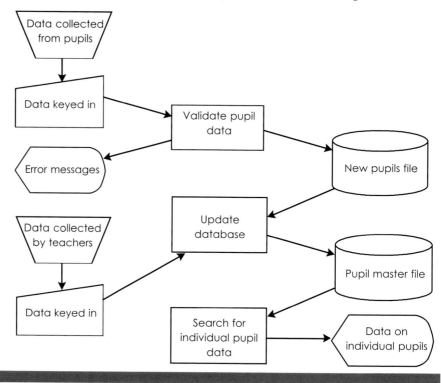

Task

Problem 3

Using the pupil database system flowchart in Figure 9.5 as a guide, draw a system flowchart to represent the following payroll system.

A company uses a computer system to process employee salaries and wages. At the start of the year employee data is transferred from the company's head office by electronic communication. Data is collected from new employees and validated as it is entered into the system. An error report is generated and any errors corrected and re-entered into the system. Data on new employees is collected by using a data-capture form, and is entered and validated as before. As part of the regular update process any data on employees leaving the company is removed to a former employees file. Each month a transaction file is produced to calculate wages and salaries. After processing the latest information is transferred to the master file. At any time during the year lists and calculations need to be printed.

You will find this easier to do if you first make a table like Table 9.1, showing input data, processing, storage and output.

9.3 Structure diagrams

The initial stage in the design of an algorithm to solve a more complex problem is to break down the problem into smaller units that can be considered as separate problems. A diagram can be used to show how this is achieved. This is known as a **structure diagram**. Structure diagrams are particularly useful when the problem has been broken down into these smaller tasks and then broken down into even smaller tasks. This method of solving a problem is known as top-down design or **stepwise refinement**. Problem 1 required you to draw a flowchart to represent the process of adding together two numbers. Compare your answer with the structure diagram in Figure 9.6.

Figure 9.6
A structure diagram

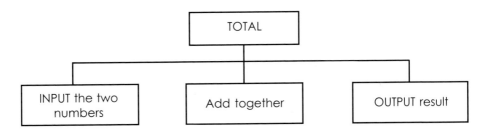

Now compare this to the recommended input–process–output method. In general terms the structure diagram can be redrawn as shown in Figure 9.7.

Figure 9.7
A generalised structure diagram

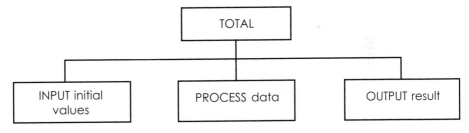

9.4 Top-down approach

Consider the example of buying the family's food for the week. The overall task is to do the weekly shopping. This can be broken down into three subtasks:

➤ write down a list of what you need to buy;

➤ do the actual shopping;

➤ take the food home and store.

Each subtask can be further subdivided into even smaller tasks, as shown in Figure 9.8.

Figure 9.8
A detailed structure diagram
showing breakdown of tasks

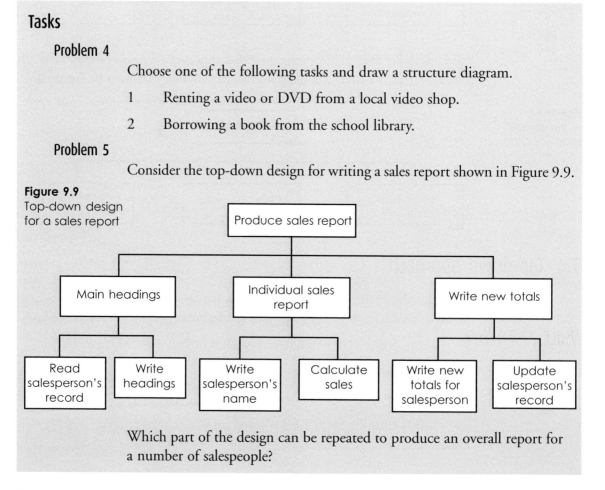

When we have broken down the problem into smaller more manageable tasks, we can devise a procedure to solve each of these smaller tasks. We can then combine these individual solutions to provide a complete solution to the larger original problem. It may also be possible to use some of these smaller solutions as part of the solution to another problem.

Tasks

Problem 4

Choose one of the following tasks and draw a structure diagram.

1   Renting a video or DVD from a local video shop.

2   Borrowing a book from the school library.

Problem 5

Consider the top-down design for writing a sales report shown in Figure 9.9.

Figure 9.9
Top-down design
for a sales report

Which part of the design can be repeated to produce an overall report for a number of salespeople?

9.5 Loops

Many problems involve a process that needs to be repeated a specific number of times. So it is useful to have a technique that performs these loops. There are a number of techniques available, such as:

➢   FOR ... NEXT

➢   WHILE ... DO

➢   REPEAT ... UNTIL.

Although these are quite similar to one another, they do have their differences.

In this book, the names of variables are written in CAPITALS to distinguish them from other code. They are displayed in **bold** type where they appear in the main text and in pseudocode. So, in the first example **NUMBER** is the name of the variable used to hold the value of the number that is input.

FOR ... NEXT loop

This is used when the loop is to be repeated a known fixed number of times. The counter is automatically increased each time the loop is performed. For example, if we want to perform a loop to add together the ten numbers from the problem in the worked example in Chapter 8, we could use:

```
For COUNT = 1 to 10
    Input NUMBER
    TOTAL = TOTAL + NUMBER
Next COUNT
```

The first time through the loop **COUNT** is equal to one, the first number is read and its value is added to the **TOTAL** to give a new **TOTAL**. Next **COUNT** adds one to **COUNT**, which is now 2, and we go back to the FOR instruction, where the value of **COUNT** is checked to see if it is still less than or equal to 10. It is still less than 10 and so the loop is repeated. This process is repeated until the value of **COUNT** is equal to 10. This is an example of an iterative loop.

WHILE ... DO loop

The WHILE ... DO loop may be used in preference to the FOR ... NEXT loop; it can also be used when we do not know how many times the loop is to be performed. The loop is ended when a certain condition is true. This condition is checked *before* starting the loop.

```
While COUNT <10 DO
    Input NUMBER
```

```
          TOTAL = TOTAL + NUMBER
          COUNT = COUNT + 1
       Endwhile
       Output TOTAL
```

It is possible for a WHILE ... DO loop never to be performed. If **COUNT** is given the value 10 before the WHILE ... DO loop is begun, when the loop checks the value of **COUNT** it finds it is not less than 10, it is equal to 10, so the condition is false and the loop is not started.

```
       COUNT = 10
       While COUNT <10 DO
          Input NUMBER
          TOTAL = TOTAL + NUMBER
          COUNT = COUNT + 1
       Endwhile
       Output TOTAL
```

REPEAT ... UNTIL loop

The REPEAT ... UNTIL loop may be used in preference to the FOR ... NEXT loop; it can also be used when we do not know how many times the loop is to be performed. The loop is ended when a certain condition is true. This condition is checked at the *end* of the loop and so a REPEAT loop always has to be performed at least once.

```
       Repeat
          Input NUMBER
             TOTAL = TOTAL + NUMBER
             COUNT = COUNT + 1
          Until COUNT = 10
       Output TOTAL
```

9.6 Selection or conditional statements

Solutions to problems often involve calculations that depend on certain conditions being true. We use selection statements IF ... THEN and CASE ... OF to test whether certain conditions have been satisfied or not.

IF ... THEN

This is often used when there is a simple test available, for example to test if a number is positive or negative.

```
       Read number
```

```
IF number > O THEN write ('positive')
      Else write ('negative')
```

The IF … THEN selection involves the use of comparisons such as

=	(equal)
<	(less than)
>	(greater than)
<=	(less than or equal)
>=	(greater than or equal).

CASE ... OF

When there is more than one simple option, it is preferable to use CASE … OF. Consider the example where a user inputs a number representing a day of the week (1 = Monday, 2 = Tuesday, etc.):

```
Case DAY of
write ('Monday')
write ('Tuesday')
write ('Wednesday')
write ('Thursday')
write ('Friday')
write ('Saturday')
write ('Sunday')
Endcase
```

9.7 Programming languages

You should be familiar with the terms 'software' and 'hardware'. Software is the general name used to describe the whole range of computer programs that allow a computer to perform specific functions. Since the hardware only operates at **machine code** level, all instructions need to be in this form before they can be carried out. The collection of codes used by the computer to perform simple operations is known as the **instruction set**; it will consist of the following basic functions together with some more specialist instructions:

➢ data transfer – the movement of data within the computer system;

➢ input–output – the movement of data to/from **peripheral devices** (such as keyboards, printers and scanners);

➢ arithmetic and logic operators – the performance of basic arithmetic and comparisons;

➢ repetition – the ability to repeat previous sets of instructions.

As hardware has developed so too has software, and programming languages now allow the programmer to concentrate on solving the problem at hand rather than on writing the actual machine code. In order to operate effectively, a programming language should include all the instruction requirements that would:

➢ control the input–output process;

➢ allow the data processing of different types of data and data structures;

➢ perform calculations/comparisons;

➢ perform selection of data following the calculations/comparisons;

➢ allow for repetition and loops;

➢ make use of subroutines and subprograms.

Computer programming languages can be divided into two types:

➢ **low-level languages** (LLL);

➢ **high-level languages** (HLL).

Low-level languages

Low-level languages (also known as machine-oriented languages) are easy for the computer to understand but difficult for the programmer. Each processor has a set of in-built instructions that is represented in **binary code** and is known as machine code. Pure machine code consists of binary numbers and is difficult to write, so other programming languages have been developed that use simple instructions (e.g. ADD, SUB, LD) to replace the binary code representing the equivalent calculator operations (e.g. add, subtract, load – the same as memory recall on a calculator). Such languages, called **assembly languages**, are easier for the programmer to understand but need to be translated into machine code before the computer can carry out the instructions. The translation is carried out by software called an **assembler**. Each assembler is written for a specific processor code or hardware and translates one assembly instruction into one machine code instruction. The assembly language instructions input is known as the **source code** and the machine code output is known as the **object code**.

High-level languages

High-level languages (also known as problem-oriented languages) have been developed for the benefit of programmers. They are easier to understand than low-level languages, many having been designed to assist in the solution of specific types of applications. For example:

➢ COBOL (Common Business Orientated Language) was developed for business applications.

> ➤ FORTRAN (FORmula TRANslation) was developed for scientific applications.

> ➤ BASIC (Beginners All-purpose Symbolic Instruction Code) and Visual BASIC were developed for general-purpose use and education.

> ➤ Other languages include LISP, LOGO, C, C++, Pascal, Java, HTML.

A high-level language consist of statements, many of which may be complex arithmetic calculations or logical comparisons. High-level languages are easier to write, easier to test and maintain, and easier to correct if errors are found. The statements are similar to instructions using the English language. These statements need much more translation and so the software needed is more complex than the assembler. One statement in a high-level language will be translated into more than one machine code instruction. Consider the simple task of adding together two numbers represented by variables B and C, and storing the answer in variable A, as shown in Table 9.2.

Table 9.2
A simple task represented in high-level and low-level languages

High-level language	Low-level language
A = B + C	LOAD C
	STORE C
	LOAD B
	STORE B
	ADD B,C
	STORE A

A high-level language program (the source code) can be translated into machine code (the object code) by using either a **compiler** or an **interpreter**. A compiler translates the entire program into machine code by the process known as compilation and, provided there are no errors in the program, produces a machine code program that can be run. This is the equivalent of translating the entire book into Arabic, rewriting it before you read it. If there are errors in the program, the compiler will produce an error report, the errors will have to be corrected and the program compiled again. An interpreter executes a high-level language program one statement at a time and will continue processing the program until it reaches the end or it detects an error. This is the equivalent of translating the book word by word but not writing down your translation, so that if you want to read the book at a later date you will have to translate it all over again.

The choice of language will depend on the actual application (see Tables 9.3 and 9.4 for a comparison). Assembly languages are particularly useful where speed is important, where there is a need to minimise memory space or where the program needs to manipulate individual memory locations.

Table 9.3 A comparison of assemblers, compilers and interpreters

Assembler	Compiler	Interpreter
Written for particular hardware	Written for particular language	Written for particular language
One instruction translates to one instruction	One instruction translates to many instructions	One instruction translates to many instructions
Translates low-level language into machine code	Translates high-level language into machine code	Translates high-level language into machine code
Translates entire program before running	Translates entire program before running	Translates program instruction by instruction until either completed or error detected

Table 9.4 A comparison of high-level and low-level languages

High-level language	Low-level language
Problem oriented	Machine oriented
One instruction translates to many instructions	One instruction translates to one instruction
Portable	Not portable
Easier to write	
Easier to test/debug	

Summary

❖ Loop techniques are helpful for solving many problems. These include:

- FOR ... NEXT – used for a fixed number of repetitions;

- WHILE ... DO – used when the exact number of repetitions is not known; condition is checked before the loop is executed;

- REPEAT ... UNTIL – used when the number of repetitions is not known; condition is checked at the end.

❖ Selection or conditional statements are used to test whether certain conditions have been satisfied. These include:

- IF ... THEN – used to test for a simple condition;

- CASE ... OF – used to test for a number of conditions.

❖ There are two types of programming language:

- Low-level languages are difficult to use and are translated to machine code by an assembler.

- High-level languages are easier to use and are translated to machine code by a compiler or an interpreter.

10 Worked examples and further exercises

The previous two chapters have explained the theory of top-down design, algorithms, pseudocode and programming languages. The only way to fully understand algorithms is to interpret a given algorithm or to devise your own working algorithm for a given problem. The chapter starts with a worked example and then this problem is extended and developed in later parts of the chapter. You will note that some words of the pseudocode appear in **bold** type. This is used to denote the names of variables or counters that are used in the algorithm. Also, when a name is more than one word, you will find that the words are joined with an underscore, '_'. You will find either or both of these techniques in the written examination paper, so getting used to them now will help you in your written examination.

Worked examples

Problem 1

A wholesale company uses a computer system to calculate the value of sales to shops. In order to calculate the total value, the system needs to look up the price of each item, the number of items sold has to be input and the value is then calculated by multiplying these two numbers. Write an algorithm to solve this problem.

Solution

Read the **unit_price**
Input the **number_of_items_sold**
Calculate **Total_Sales** = **unit_price** multiplied by **number_of_items_sold**
Output **Total_Sales**

Problem 2

The wholesale company also needs to make sure that each shop is an authorised customer, so for each order the system needs to check whether the shop is an existing customer or a new customer. (Existing customers will have a **customer_id**.) If it is a new customer, then the order is placed in a Queries file. Also, a check needs to be made to see if an existing customer is still allowed to place orders or whether the customer's account has been stopped. Write an algorithm to solve this problem.

Solution

```
Input the customer_id
Read customer_id and customer_status from Customer file
IF customer_id does not exist THEN place order in Queries file
IF customer_status = 'stop' THEN place order in Queries file
Process order
```

Problem 3

The orders have to be processed for a number of customers until there are no more unfilled orders. The Order file contains details of the **customer_id**s and the number of items purchased. **Sales_tax** has to be added to the **net_price** at the rate of 15% to give the **sales_price**. Write an algorithm to solve this problem.

Solution

```
WHILE there are no more unfilled orders DO
Read the next order
Read customer_id and number_of_items_sold from the Customer file
Calculate net_price = unit_price multiplied by number_of_items_sold
Calculate sales_tax = net_price multiplied by 15%
Calculate sales_price = net_price + sales_tax
Output sales_price
```

Example questions

The following questions are related to the wholesale company discussed in the worked examples. Write algorithms to solve the following problems.

1   Input a **customer_id**, **item_number** and **number_of_items_sold**. Details of stock (**unit_price** and **quantity_in_stock**) are contained in the Stock file. Check to see if an item is out of stock.

2   Process a number of orders from the Order file and use the Stock file to print those orders where the item is out of stock.

3   Input a **customer_id**, **item_number** and **number_of_items_sold**. Details of stock (**unit_price** and **quantity_in_stock**) are contained in the Stock file. Check to see if an item is out of stock. If the item is in stock, then reduce the **quantity_in_stock** by the **number_of_items_sold**.

4   The company offers the following discounts for large orders.

Value (excluding sales_tax)	Discount
Less than $100	No discount
$100–$199.99	3%
$200–$399.99	7%
$400–$699.99	10%
$700 and over	15%

Use the CASE … OF construct to output the final **selling_price** (excluding **sales_tax**).

5   The company wishes to send advertising material to its customers who have placed an order in the last 12 months. The required date is input, the Customer file is checked to find the date of last order and the customer details are written to the Mailshot file if the last order date is on or after this required date.

6   The company places an extra condition of the last order being $200 or more. Rewrite your answer to question 5 to include this extra condition.

7   The Stock file contains **stock_id**, **stock_description**, **quantity_in_stock**, **reorder_level** (the number when an item should be reordered if the **quantity_in_stock** falls below the **reorder_level**), **reorder_quantity** (how many will be reordered) and **supplier_id**. The names and addresses of the suppliers are contained in a separate Supplier file.

Write an algorithm that will produce a report showing which items need to be reordered, how many and the supplier's name and address.

8   Look at the following algorithm:

```
Counter = 0
input Character
WHILE Character is not a full stop DO
    IF Character is not a space then
        Counter = Counter + 1
    ENDIF
    input Character
ENDWHILE
output Character
```

What character will end the WHILE construct?

What is the purpose of the **Counter** variable?

Copy the following table and use it to record the values obtained while carrying out the algorithm using the following input. What is the final output?

Input: **See me later.**

Character	Counter
	0
S	1
e	2
e	3
space	3
m	
e	
space	
l	
a	
t	
e	
r	
.	

What is the purpose of the algorithm?

Why will the algorithm fail to work on the following input?
See me at lunchtime

Why will the algorithm fail to work on the following input?
The average mark is 4.5

9   Look at the following algorithm:

```
value = 0
   new_value = 0
   input value
   input next_value
   WHILE new_value is not equal to zero DO
       IF new_value is greater than value
THEN value is equal to new_value
ENDIF
input next_value
ENDWHILE
output value
```

What is the output using 1, 3, 2, 2, 4, 5, 6, 2, 0?

What is the purpose of the algorithm?

10   A microprocessor is used to control a washing machine. The microprocessor calculates the time needed using the weight of the clothes, which is to be input by the user. Write an algorithm to describe the processing.

11   A school library keeps its students' details in a master file. Students are issued with magnetic cards. When a student wants to borrow a book, the card is swiped through a card reader. The library's computer first checks to see if the student is allowed to borrow another book. If they are, a loan code is issued to the library. Design an algorithm to show this data processing.

12   Using pseudocode, or otherwise, design an algorithm that will accept a list of five numbers and output the total of these five numbers.

13   Using pseudocode, or otherwise, design an algorithm that will accept any list of numbers and output the total of these numbers.

14   This algorithm grades candidates on marks out of hundred:

```
input MARK
    case MARK of
    0–19: GRADE = Fail
    20–39: GRADE = Pass
    40–69: GRADE = Merit
    70–100: GRADE = Distinction
    otherwise MARK = –1
Endcase
IF MARK = –1 THEN
    print 'Not a valid mark' else output GRADE, 'Grade'
```

(a)   Dry run the algorithm for each of the following data and write down the corresponding output.

   20, 45, 79, 125

(b)   Rewrite the algorithm so that it could be used for a class of 30 students.

15   Write an algorithm to accept the value of each sale at a supermarket till and output the number of sales and the total value of the sales.

16   Write an algorithm to accept the value of each sale or refund at a shop point-of-sale (POS) terminal and output the number of sales, the number of refunds, the total value of refunds and the total

value of the sales. (*Hint*: Refunds can be represented as a negative sale – a refund of $5 would be represented as an input of –5.)

17   Design an algorithm so that it will accept any number of numbers, the input is terminated by a rogue value and the output is the total of all the numbers input except the rogue value.

18   Read this algorithm:

```
Input VALUE_1, VALUE_2
    IF VALUE_1 < VALUE_2 THEN
        T = VALUE_1
        VALUE_1 = VALUE_2
        VALUE_2 = T
    Endif
Output VALUE_1, VALUE_2
```

(a)   Write down the output if the following two numbers are input: 41, 138.

(b)   What is the purpose of the algorithm?

19   Design an algorithm for the following process to calculate an employee's weekly pay. To calculate weekly pay, input the number of hours worked and the pay rate per hour. Multiply the number of hours worked by the pay rate for hours worked less than or equal to 40. For any hours worked over 40 the pay rate is increased by 50%.

20   A computer program is being written to input the names and examination marks of 4,000 students. Marks are graded as DISTINCTION for marks over 80%, MERIT for marks over 60%, PASS for marks of 30% or more and FAIL for marks of less than 30%. The solution should also count the number of students gaining each particular grade. The output is required to show the name and grade for each student together with the name of each grade and the number of students obtaining each grade.

21   Describe the differences between high-level and low-level languages.

22   What is the connection between object code and source code?

23   Describe the differences between an assembler and a compiler.

24   Why is a high-level language translated into machine code? Describe the differences between an interpreter and an assembler.

Extension work

1   Describe two features of a high-level language that are not found in a low-level language.

2   In which situation is it better to use a low-level language rather than a high-level language?

3   Using a suitable example, explain how the CASE ... OF construct works. Show how this could also be achieved by the use of a nested IF ... THEN construct.

4   Distinguish between an assembler and a compiler.

5   Camm Publishing uses more than one printing company to print its books. The main criteria to be used are the number of copies to be printed and whether or not the book is to be printed in colour. If the book is to be printed in colour then it goes to Abbs Printing, except that if the book is needed within seven days it goes to Babbs printing. If the book is to be printed in black and white only then it goes to Babbs Printing, but they can only print a maximum of ten thousand copies. So if more than ten thousand copies are needed, it goes to Cabbs Printing.

Design an algorithm to decide which printer is to be used. Test your algorithm with the following orders:

(a)   1,000 copies of a colour book needed in four days.

(b)   20,000 copies of a black-and-white book needed in two weeks.

(c)   9,000 copies of a black-and-white book needed in two days.

(d)   9,000 copies of a black-and-white book needed in two weeks.

6   What is the purpose of the following pseudocode?

```
Enter names
REPEAT
    Set swapped to NO
    Look at first pair of names
    REPEAT
        WHILE names out of order DO
        SWAP names
        Set swapped to YES
        End
        Look at next pair of names
```

```
                UNTIL no more names
            UNTIL swapped is NO
            Output names
```

Test this algorithm with the following data: Ahmed, Ikram, Peter, Ferhan, Nizar.

4 Software and data organisation

11 | Software

Learning objectives

When you have finished this chapter you will be able to:

❖   state the difference between applications and operating system software;

❖   identify uses for and characteristics of generic applications software;

❖   understand how computer models are used to simulate situations.

11.1 Definition

IT1b

Software consists of programs, routines and procedures (together with their associated documentation) that can be run on a computer system.

Think of the 'hard' bits of the computer and then remember that they are just metal and plastic. Something has to tell these components what to do to make them work like a computer. This is the job of the software. Notice in the definition that we mentioned documentation (we discussed documentation in Chapters 6 and 8). Software is useless unless you know how to use it, and it is the documentation that tells you how to use it, so the documentation must be included. Nowadays, the documentation is likely to be part of the program as 'onscreen help', but it is still there.

There are two types of software:

applications software, which allows us to use the computer to do something useful, from playing games to word processing to monitoring the condition of patients in a hospital;

operating system software, which makes the computer work and gets it to the state where it is ready to run our programs (this type of software is covered in detail in Chapter 14).

11.2 Types of applications software

IT4a, f;
7.1a;
7.2a, b

When thinking about applications software there are two questions to bear in mind:

➢ What does the software do?

➢ What is the software used for?

The best way of learning about software, and answering these two questions, is to use it, as you will be doing in your practical lessons.

Questions in theory papers are likely to give you a situation and ask what software should be used in such a situation; you will also be asked to justify your choice. Remember that when you are answering the questions, you should not use the name of a particular brand of software, you should always give a type of software. So, 'Word' would be wrong, because the answer should have been 'a word processor'.

Communication using hard copy

Included in this type of software are word processors and **desktop publishing (DTP)** programs. There used to be a clear distinction between these two types of software: word processors were used like typewriters to produce letters and other text-based documents while DTP was used to create pages for publications that required more complex layout, perhaps with columns of the text wrapped around **graphics**. There is still a distinction between the two, but it is much less rigid now. Word processors will do most of the things that DTP used to do and there is no reason why a letter cannot be written using a DTP program. We wrote this book using a word processor and the publisher imported it into a DTP program to arrange it and add the diagrams. Newspaper reporters type their stories straight into the paper using DTP. This shows a difference between the types of software: word processors are used for creating the text documents, whereas DTP is used to manipulate sets of documents, both graphic and text, to produce a finished article.

Other communications software

There is a lot of software that allows communication by electronic means.

Presentation software

Presentation software is used to make and give computer-controlled electronic presentations. Such presentations are usually given to groups. For example, a teacher might use the software with a class learning a new topic, or a sales director might use it to give a presentation to a group of potential customers. Most presentation software lets you construct your presentation using text, graphics and animation, including morphing (gradually transforming one image into the next). You can also add sound – perhaps music or even a recorded commentary. Sound, graphics, animation and text are called media, so a program that allows you to use a mixture of these media to convey the information is called a multimedia package. Most software is multimedia to some extent.

Internet and email software

Everyone has heard of the Internet and most of us have used it at one time or another. When using it, we may think to ourselves how wonderful it is to have so much information available, but rarely do we think about the software that is needed to give us access to all that information. This is an example of communications software that we do not need to understand – we simply have it on our computers.

Software that we use on the Internet includes:

➢   web browsers, which allow access to the Internet;

➢   search engines, which help us to find information;

➢   email programs, which allow us to send and receive electronic mail.

You will have used these in your practical lessons. Theory questions will be about how to use the Internet. They may ask about how to use search engines to find articles on a particular topic and about the need to refine searches because the search engine will find too much. They may also ask about the facilities available when using electronic mail, such as the ability to forward mail to other addresses, to attach documents to a message, to encrypt messages if necessary, and to save messages in your own files.

Documents can be sent by email as well as messages. If they are confidential, they can be protected both by passwords and by encryption. **Electronic signatures** (also known as **digital signatures**) are sometimes used as part of the encryption process. They allow the recipient to make sure that the documents are genuine and that they came from the right place. The way they work is as follows. The sender includes a message (the signature) that is encrypted. When the message gets to the recipient, the signature is decoded. If it makes sense, this means that the signature was encrypted properly and so the message must have come from the genuine person. If the message had come from anyone, else they wouldn't have been able to encrypt the message properly, so the recipient would know the document was a fraud.

Of course, documents can be sent far more easily than this – even sending them over a phone line through a fax machine counts as an electronic means and is therefore part of this course, though such vulnerable methods of communication would not be used for important messages.

The simplest way to use the Internet or email services is through an ordinary telephone line. The signal produced by the computer cannot be sent down a phone line as it is, so a special device called a modem is needed to change the signal into one that can. Another modem is needed at the other end to change the signal back into one that the computer can process. There are other means of communicating that are much faster than the phone lines. Because they are so much faster, much more information can travel down them in a given time and more than one communication can be sent at a time. This makes **video conferencing** possible, in which several people in different locations can have a discussion and see each other at the same time. Imagine a business with offices all over the world – instead of flying all the bosses to one place for a meeting they can stay where they are and hold a meeting electronically.

Extension work

Find out about some services available in your area. They will probably quote the bandwidth of their service. Most people think that the higher the **bandwidth**, the faster the messages are sent. This is not true.

1   Try to find out what a higher bandwidth means.

2   Can you see a similarity with the number of stations that you can pick up on your radio and the problem of interference when you are trying to tune it in?

Mobile phones are another example of equipment that can send and receive data very conveniently.

3   Consider the advantages and disadvantages of having mobile phones freely available.

4   Does the availability of phones that will take digital pictures and instantly transmit them change any of your thoughts about advantages and disadvantages?

Another type of software used in communications is **website authoring software**. This is a bit like DTP software, except that the end result is a website rather than something printed. A successful website depends on good planning. This is even more important than the choice of software to be used to produce it.

Things to be considered include:

- the type of information that needs to be displayed;
- how many pages there will be;
- how the pages will be connected;
- what colour scheme should be used;
- what links there should be to other sites.

The actual production of the site is fairly easy because the software virtually does it for you – the difficult bit is the planning.

Look at some sites of companies on the Internet. Criticise them using the following questions.

5   How easy is it to navigate them?

6   How easy is it to find a particular piece of information about the company?

7   Do the pages of the site look uniform? (Do they use the same colours, design and layout? Does every page display the company logo?)

8   How could you improve the site?

11.3 Data-handling software

IT7.1b

The major use of computers is not calculations or communications, but storing and handling data. More processor power is used around the world in looking after and manipulating stored data than all the other processing put together. What do we mean by data handling? It is the ability of the computer to store, search and find data. Your school used to keep student records on paper. Each student's details were stored in a folder that was kept, along with all the other students' folders, in filing cabinets. Nowadays your school probably stores your details on a computer system.

Why do we use computers for this? If a teacher wants details about student Raiza Siddiqi, the computer has to be turned on, the correct software has to be loaded and then information has to be entered so that the correct student is found. It used to be a lot faster just to look in the filing cabinet and get out her file, and it was far cheaper. But would it be quicker if the teacher wanted details of all the students doing Computing? That would depend on whether paper lists of who was doing which subject were kept as part of the old system. What about if we wanted to know which students were in room D3 on a Tuesday afternoon? What about wanting a list of all students who attained a grade B or higher in their last exams? Now the problems are getting immense. In the old system, someone would have to go through all the information and pick out the students who fit the criteria. This is possible, but it takes a lot of time. That is what database software on the computer is so good at: doing simple searching jobs very quickly.

Imagine a teacher in another teaching block who needs to see Raiza's record. The teacher does not need to walk over to the admin section and search for Raiza's record; they simply go to a computer terminal and access it from where they are. In a business, that terminal could be anywhere in the world.

11.4 Spreadsheets

IT7.1e

Another type of data-handling software is the **spreadsheet**. Typically a spreadsheet is like a big piece of paper that has been divided into rectangles (called cells) into which we can put data. The spreadsheet stores not only the data values but also the position of the data on the sheet. So, for example, the third cell down in the second column might store '3'; if the third row down is 'March' and second column is '2nd', the single value '3' might mean that there were three bookings on the second of March, or there were three people absent on the second of March.

Really, a spreadsheet is just like a database: they are both designed to store and manipulate data. The difference used to be that only spreadsheets allowed users to do arithmetic and only databases allowed searches to be made on the data, but both types of software can perform both functions now. While it is important that you are aware of these differences, and mentioning them will earn you marks in an exam question, a more important difference now is the power of a spreadsheet to predict future trends by using mathematical formulae in computer models. You will have used a spreadsheet like this yourselves, probably in your maths work, with questions like 'If the following relationships are true, what will the result be in 2 years time?'

Spreadsheets can also be used to do simulations. If a situation is too dangerous or too expensive to do in real life, a spreadsheet can be used to predict what will happen. For instance, there are not many pilots who would be willing to fly a plane to discover the answer to the question 'If this aircraft is made to corner very tightly, will the wings stay on?', so a spreadsheet is produced instead. All the measurements of the strains and stresses on the wings are added to the spreadsheet, along with details of the mathematical formulae that show how the measurements are all connected. The spreadsheet can then predict whether or not the wings will stay on. This is called a model – not a wooden model, but a mathematical model. It doesn't look like a plane, just a lot of numbers, but if you are clever with spreadsheets, it can tell you more about what the plane will do in real life than a wooden model ever could.

11.5 CAD/CAM

CAD stands for **computer-aided design**. This is exactly what it says: the computer is used to help people design things. Computers are ideal instruments for design work compared with pencil and paper. CAD is especially useful for designing things like circuit boards and other electronic circuits because they tend to be made up of standard parts (the drawings for each of these can be kept in a library) and the parts are repeated many times, which can be done on the computer by a simple copy and paste operation. Another advantage of using the computer is that the circuits work according to very simple and strict rules, so the design can be tested before it is actually produced. The design can be amended easily, exact measurements can be made and perfect shapes, such as circles, can be drawn. The design can be stored on the hard disk, it can be sent from one place to another as an email attachment and lots of copies can be made. When the final design has been produced, it can be passed to computer-controlled machines, which can then make the product automatically from the design. This second stage is known as **CAM**, or **computer-aided manufacture**.

11.6 Software packages and their integration

Much of the software that we have discussed in this chapter allows a certain amount of internal integration. For example, DTP programs often come with basic graphics and other software needed to produce a document – this is all part of the package. However, we also expect our DTP software to let us import a spreadsheet or a picture from a painting program to illustrate a point. When we have finished producing a page, we also expect to be able to export it to the website authoring software that is being used to produce a website. This ability of all the different software types to talk to each other is not universal, and software that will allow this is known as **integrated software**.

Most computer users find that the readily available software that can be bought is quite adequate for what they want. This is called **off-the-shelf software** because it can be picked up off the shelf in a shop. Much of this software can be confusing because it probably does far more than necessary. Fortunately, it can be made to hide all the bits that a user does not need, and the bits they do want to use can be made easy to understand. For example, the input and output screens can be simplified and the data can be made easy to find – it is even possible to make the screens come up in corporate colours. This is called customising the software because it is being altered to suit the needs of one customer. It is done using little programs called **macros**.

Sometimes it is necessary to have a piece of software specially written to solve a particular problem. This **custom-written software** will be very expensive and will probably have far more errors than off-the shelf software (it won't have been used so much so fewer errors will have been found). However, it will do exactly what is required.

11.7 Data logging

IT7.1c

Data can be collected in many ways. If a person asks lots of people how tall they are, they are collecting data. A thermometer on the wall in an office is collecting data about what the temperature is. Much of the data that is collected is not for putting into a computer, and a lot will be discarded and never used. Sometimes the data is fed straight into a computer. Perhaps the thermometer is telling a computerised heating system how hot it is in the office; the data would be passed straight to the computer so that it can decide whether or not to turn up the air conditioning. Perhaps the intention is to take readings over the course of a day so that we can gauge how well the system works. In this example, the data does not need to be sent to the computer for 24 hours, but it is still important to collect the data all the time. We say that the data needs to be 'logged' before the temperature changes. It will then be stored, normally on a tape, and later it will all be sent to the computer together. This whole process is called **data logging**. You may have used data logging when you were doing experiments in science. For example, perhaps you used data-logging equipment to take regular measurements of the temperature of an experiment and then input the data to a computer so that a graph of temperature loss could be drawn.

Extension work

When a device is used to measure temperature electronically, it is not called a thermometer, it is called a **thermistor**.

1   Think of situations in which a thermistor would be preferred to a thermometer.

There is a problem when some measurements are being taken, caused by the type of data that is being input to the computer – we will discuss this in Chapters 12 and 13.

Imagine an automatic weather station and the data that needs to be collected.

2   How often should readings be taken?

3   How often should the readings be transmitted back to the head office of the weather bureau?

4   How much data needs to be collected each time?

5   Would a floppy disk be a sensible place to store the logged data?

Example questions

1   A small manufacturing business invests in a computer system and an integrated software package.

(a)   Explain what is meant by an integrated software package.   (3)

(b)   State four different programs that you would expect to be in the software package and explain how each program would be used. (8)

Suggested answers

(a)   Software means the instructions that make the computer produce something.

Package means that there are a number of individual pieces of software and that everything, as well as a user guide, is included.

Integrated means that the different parts of the package can communicate with each other and share data.

Notes: Notice that there is an answer for each of the three words. A common error in answers to a question like this is not providing enough information to allow the examiner to give you the marks. Always take notice of the number of marks for the question.

(b)   • Word processor, to produce letters for sending to customers and suppliers.

• Desktop publisher, to produce posters and brochures to advertise the company's products.

• Spreadsheet, to keep the company accounts / to provide invoices for the customers.

• Database, to keep details of customers / suppliers / stock.

• Web authoring, to produce a website to advertise the company.

Notes: The question said that it was a 'small' company. That word is there for a reason. Because it is small, the company would almost certainly be buying an off-the-shelf package. Notice that generic terms like 'word processor' are used, not names of the proprietary brands. The programs given in our answer are just examples; there are others that would also be acceptable, such as email software for communication with suppliers. As long as you come up with something sensible you will get the mark. You do need to be careful, though, as you don't know how far you can stray from the obvious answers and still get a mark. For example, what about CAD? Would that be classed as part of an integrated package? And if it is, what about CAM? The safe thing to do is stick to the obvious answers. We have used ' / ' to indicate alternative words or phrases that would gain the mark.

2(a)   Explain why off-the-shelf software is turned into customised software. (4)

(b)   Describe how this customisation is done.   (4)

Suggested answers

(a)   ◆ Off-the-shelf software is generic. It is designed to do many things / solve many problems.

◆ Most of these things / solutions do not relate to the business in which it is to be used.

◆ The large number of options in off-the-shelf software will be confusing / will increase the need for training of personnel.

◆ Customisation allows input screens to be created according to input documents rather than new input documents having to be created to match the software.

◆ It also allows output screens to reflect the company (by use of colours and logo).

Notes: Again, notice the large number of marks available. You don't have to come up with all the mark points to get the marks, but you do need to get at least four points because there are four marks. It is quite usual for there to be extra marks available because it would be unfair to expect you to come up with the full answer in the exam. This is not always true, but normally there are more mark points than marks for a question. Write your answer as bullet points or number them. Notice that the question is not so much about the software as the typical place where it would be used. A genuine exam question would probably tell you about the business that it would be used in.

(b)   ◆ A systems analyst studies the organisation and works out the types of input and output required.

◆ The analyst also studies the abilities of the staff and gauges the level of training that will be required.

- A programmer uses the macros / wizards within the software / to produce designs from the analyst as the default for the system.

- All other tools are hidden.

- User (and technical) documentation is hidden.

Notes: There are lots of mark points, but if you are going to get full marks it is necessary to think in terms of Section 2 and include information about the systems analyst's part in this. And don't forget the documentation.

Summary

❖ There are two types of software. Operating system software controls the hardware of a system while applications software allows the user to do something useful with the computer.

❖ There are many different types of applications software for different purposes. The types include:

- word processing

- DTP

- presentation software

- graphics

- website authoring

- database

- spreadsheet

- CAD/CAM

- data logging.

❖ Off-the-shelf software is readily available, it can then be tailored to the requirements of the organisation that has bought it. Sometimes software has to be specially written to solve a specific problem.

12 Data

Learning objectives

When you have finished this chapter you will be able to:

❖   explain the distinction between data and information;

❖   understand the use of coded data;

❖   describe the difference between analogue and digital data;

❖   name two types of input checks: verification and validation;

❖   explain the difference between and the relationships within: file, record, field, item, key;

❖   outline different file organisations and their uses;

❖   understand that data is stored in a computer according to type so that the computer can identify where and in what form the data should be stored.

12.1 Information and data

Most people are very lazy about using the terms 'data' and 'information'. They tend to be used to mean the same thing, whereas there is a clear difference between them. Data consists of values stored inside the computer. It doesn't mean very much; most of the time it is stored as **coded data**, which we human beings would find difficult to understand anyway. Information is data that has been given some added value that makes it understandable. For instance, '3' and 'L' are both data. They are obviously different from each other and they are also different from 6 or M, but they are meaningless. However, add '$' to the number to give '$3' and suddenly the 3 means something. Similarly, if someone tells you the letter is on a shirt, then 'L' probably means large and 'M' means medium. The values now have a meaning. So, information is data in a context that gives it meaning.

12.2 Data collection and preparation

IT4b,c

Computer systems need data to be able to do anything worthwhile. Without data a system has nothing to process and consequently cannot produce an output. Data that is to be input to a computer needs to be collected. This data-collection stage has been covered in Chapter 11 and will be returned to in Chapter 13.

Data that is collected is sometimes not in a suitable form to be entered into a computer system. A simple example is a date of birth, which may be in any of the following formats:

18 November 1983;

18th of November 1983;

November 18th, 1983;

the 18th day of November 1983;

18/11/83 (this is the way a British person would write it);

11/18/83 (this would be from an American – they always put the month first);

83/11/18 (this is how an Australian would write it).

How would you write down your date of birth?

Imagine that a question on a data-capture form asked for the person's date of birth. The answers would be in a different format depending on where the person was from. Before this data is input to a computer system it needs to be prepared so that all the dates are in the same form, otherwise unexpected things will happen in the processing.

While we are thinking about dates, what does 181183 mean? It could be a representation of the 18th of November 1983, but it only represents that date if we follow certain rules. It is certainly a lot simpler to key in and because there are fewer characters there will be fewer mistakes made. Also, because it is a lot shorter, it will use up far less space in the computer storage. What has happened is that the data has been coded. That does not mean that the data has been made secret, everyone can work out what date it represents, but it is a shortened version of what is represented. Another example would be using M and F for male and female.

In the second block of extension work in Chapter 11 we mentioned collecting data in a weather station for processing in a computer. Like date of birth, this type of data also needs to be prepared before it can be processed. When a temperature is measured, it can be any value, and may include several decimal places. Data like this is called **analogue data**. Analogue data is **physical data**, such as temperature, length, weight and other measurements from the real world. Computers do not like analogue measurements. They want separate values that go up in steps – this is known as **digital data**. For instance, a height could be 1.2345 cm, but a computer may only accept numbers that go up in hundredths, so it will only accept 1.23 cm. Measurements that are analogue must be converted into digital data before a computer can use them. This is another form of data preparation.

12.3 Data input and checking

The study of data input includes the study of the hardware that is needed to input the data; this will be covered in Chapter 13.

When data is input to a computer system, it is important to make sure that no errors are made. There is no point in spending a large amount of money on the most modern equipment and the best software if the wrong data is put into the system. There are two types of checking that should be done on data input to a system:

➢   data **verification**

➢   data validation.

They sound very similar but are actually totally different, so be careful.

Data verification is checking to make sure that what was input to the system was what was meant to be input. In other words, no typing errors. If someone has written on a data form that their date of birth is 18/11/83 and the input operator keys in 19/11/83, a mistake has been made. There are two ways to stop this happening:

➢   read through what has been keyed in to check that no silly mistakes have been made;

➢   have two people key the data in, then the computer can compare the two inputs and if they are not the same it can ask for the data to be keyed in again.

The method that is used depends on the application and how important the data input is. If it is just the date of birth of a student in a school, it doesn't matter a lot, so checking by reading through will be enough. If it is someone's bank account details, it is very important, so the expense of two people inputting the same data is probably worth it.

Data validation is checking to make sure that the right sort of data has been input. This is done by the computer system itself, following a set of rules that it has been given. For instance, if you want a computer to check that a date of birth is a valid date, you could tell it that the first two digits must be a number less than 32. When the data is keyed in, the computer will check the first two digits; if '35' has been entered, the computer knows this is wrong because it breaks the rule. There are a number of possible validation checks; this one is called a range check because the computer checks to see if the value is in a particular range. Another is called a character check. In our example you could tell the computer to make sure all the characters used are either digits or slashes (/). If '18/e1/83' is entered, it will break the rule and the computer will know it is wrong. A length check will make sure that there are eight characters while a format check will make sure that there are six digits in pairs split up by slashes.

Notice that despite the two types of check being done it is still possible that a piece of data is wrong. The person who was asked for their date of birth might have lied in the first place, and no amount of care or checking of the input will then make it right.

Extension work

1   Think about the different pieces of information that your school holds about you. Try to find out what measures are taken to make sure that the data stored is as accurate as it can be.

2   Consider the database software that you use. It probably has some inbuilt methods of validation that you can use. Make a list of these validation methods and make sure you can use them.

3   Find out what is meant by an 'input mask' and try using it for input of data to a database.

When long numbers that don't alter, such as barcodes or ISBNs on books, are input to a computer, another method is used to check that they have been read properly. When a barcode is scanned at a supermarket checkout, the computer does some arithmetic on all the digits represented by the barcode except one. This arithmetic is designed so that the answer will always be the single digit that is not used in the arithmetic. If the answer is not this digit, it means the other numbers have not been read properly. This is what happens at the checkout when the barcode scanner doesn't beep – the barcode has not been read properly and the arithmetic does not give the right answer.

4   Is this a validation check or a verification check?

5   What does the checkout operator do if the barcode is so damaged that the scanner will not read it?

12.4 File organisation and techniques

Consider the set of data about students in a school shown in Table 12.1.

Table 12.1
A sample of student data

IT5c

ID number	Name	Sex	Form	Tutor
18759	Noah Amu	M	4AD	Ms Arif
36729	Razia Mukadam	F	3JU	Mr Ali
51734	Shan Faizan	F	6YD	Ms Syed
51736	Ahmad Makhtar	M	3JU	Mr Ali

This is only a small section of all the students in the school and only a small amount of the data held on each one. The full set of data would fill this book.

The full set of data about all the students is called the file. It is too big to do very much with and finding any information would be very time-consuming, so the file is split up into sets of data about one thing.

These sets of data are called **records**. In this case each row of data is a record.

Each record contains lots of pieces of data. Each piece of data is called an **item** and is stored in a space called a **field**. Notice that all the records have the same fields, but not necessarily the same items. One of these items, and the field that it is in, is special because no other record can have the same item. This is called the key or the **key field** (it is sometimes called the 'record key' too – don't worry, they all mean the same thing). The key is the item that is used to identify which record is being used.

In this example:

➢   All the information about all the students in the school is the file.

➢   All the data about one student is a record, so four records are shown.

➢   Each piece of data is an item, so 'Shan Faizan' is an item and 'Mr Ali' is an item. Twenty items are shown in the table, though there will be a lot more.

➢   Each column is a field, so 'ID number' is a field, so is 'Form'.

➢   The key is 'ID number' because it is the only field that contains items that can never be the same as another item. It might be tempting to use 'Name' as the key, because all the names are different. However, it cannot be guaranteed that they will be always different. Think about your school – it would be surprising if everyone had a different name.

➢ Some fields do not mean what they say. Noah is not an M! He is a male. We all know that M stands for male, so we not are trying to keep it secret, it is just that M is easier to type in. This is an example of a coded field.

This has split the file into smaller parts that can now be searched.

Notice that these records are in order of the key. This sort of file is called a **sequential file** because the records are in sequence. Records are often stored in order of the key, either numerically or alphabetically, because this creates a file that is a lot easier to use and find things in.

If the file is in no particular order, or just in the order that the records were input (i.e. chronological order), it is called a **serial file**. Serial files are not very useful because they make it so difficult to find any information. They are kept when the file is not going to be used immediately. For example, a record of all the transactions that take place in a shop will be kept as a serial file until the end of the day, when it may be converted to a sequential file in alphabetical order of items that were bought.

An alternative to converting a serial file to a sequential file is to create an index and allow the records to be kept randomly on the surface of a disk. Any record can be found without having to look through all of them, simply by going to the index and looking up the key in the index to find the location of the record. This is called a **direct access file** and it is used in files where it is not possible to predict the order in which the records will be needed, such as the product records for the checkout in the supermarket.

Three types of maintenance are necessary in most files:

➢ Updates or amendments to a record – For example, the form for each student will change at the end of the year. There is no need to key in all the other data again, it is simply a matter of changing that one piece of data in each record.

➢ Insertions – For example, if a new student arrives during the school year, a new record will need to be inserted. If the file is stored sequentially this will mean rewriting large parts of the file in order to create the space to put the new record in. If the file is a direct access file, it is only necessary to change the index.

➢ Deletions – For example, if a student transferred to another school during the school year, their record would need to be taken out of the file.

Extension work

1 How would the file be altered if a student left the school during the year? Think about the effect on the student file if it was stored sequentially and if it was stored as a direct access file.

2 Another field on each student's record is their age. What are the implications of this for updating the file? Can you think of a more satisfactory alternative?

3 A teacher gets married and changes her name. Explain how this would affect the file and how the updating can be done. Can you think of a way of doing the updating that does not require looking at every record?

4 The text suggests that random files and direct access files are the same thing, which is fine for this level of work, but they are actually different. Can you find out what the difference is?

12.5 Reason for having different data types

Data cannot just be input to a computer. In order to understand why we cannot just type it in we must understand a little about how computers store data. Data is coded when it is input to a computer system. So, when I key in 'A', the computer changes it into a code and it is the code that is stored. When the character needs to be output, the computer looks up the code in a table and changes it back to an 'A', which is then output. The code for 'A' is 01000001. Don't be worried by this, we never see these codes. Similarly, when I type in the number '65', the computer cannot store it, so it has to change it into a code that it can store. The code for '65' is 01000001. Now there is a problem – the codes for A and 65 are the same! When the computer changes 01000001 back into a character so that it can be output, does it choose A or 65? This problem can only be solved if the computer knows what sort of characters the codes were made to stand for in the first place. This is the reason why we must tell the computer what sort of data we are giving it before the data is input. When you are programming and want to input a number or do a calculation, you have to tell the computer what sort of numbers you want to use. When you are using database software and want to store an item in a field, the computer needs to know what sort of items go in that field before they are input.

12.6 Different data types

Numbers

There are two types of number that have to be identified:

➤ whole numbers, which don't contain decimals (the proper name for them is 'integers');

➤ numbers that include decimals (these are called 'reals').

It is important for the computer to know if the data is going to be an integer so it does not waste space allowing for storage of the decimal part of the number. If a calculation is going to be done that divides one integer by another, though, the answer might include a decimal part, so the computer has to be aware that the answer needs to be a different type of data.

Integers are used for things like a person's age, whereas a real would have to be used for their height (1.76 m).

Currency

One set of real numbers is used so often that it has a special data type of its own: 'currency'. This is used to tell the computer that the data is a real number that has a limit of two decimal places and will have a unit with it, such as $ or £.

Date

Another type of data that looks as though it is all numbers is 'date'. Dates are often input to computers as three sets of two digits separated by slashes. The computer needs to know that it is a date so that it can do validation checks to make sure the right sort of data has been input (see subsection 12.3 above).

Text

Most data that is input to a computer consists of characters from the keyboard. This is data that has no hidden meaning (like the first two digits of a date must be between 1 and 31) and it is not going to be used in calculations. It just needs to be stored. Data from the keyboard that is treated like this is called 'text' (for obvious reasons) or 'alphanumeric', because it can be letters of the alphabet or numbers, or sometimes it is called 'character', because it consists of characters on the keyboard.

Boolean data

Some data is very different from all other data because it can only be one of two characters – such data is called **Boolean data**. An example of this is 'Y' or

'N' for a yes or no answer to a question. Sometimes data like this is used as the answer to a simple logical question like 'Is the data input bigger than 31?' There are only two possible answers. If the reason for the question was to see if the number could be a day of the month and the answer was 'Y', the computer might have been programmed to output 'You can have no more than 31 days in a month'. Boolean data is used a lot in validation checks as the answer to these simple questions. When it is used like this, it is sometimes called **logical data**.

Example questions

1   Consider the part of a file shown in Table 12.1.

(a)   State the data types that would be used for each of the five fields shown, explaining your choice.   (10)

(b)   Suggest extra fields that could be sensibly stored in the file that would be examples of the other data types mentioned above.   (6)

Suggested answers

(a)   ID number is alphanumeric – it consists of characters from the keyboard and would not be used as a number.

Name is alphanumeric – it consists of characters from the keyboard.

Sex is a Boolean data type – it has only two possibilities, M or F.

Form is alphanumeric – it consists of a code made up of keys on the keyboard

Tutor is alphanumeric – it is a person's name that consists of letters of the alphabet.

Notes: Sometimes numbers look as if they should be stored as integers, but they are not. A good test is to ask what the answer would mean if two of these 'numbers' were added together. If the answer would not make sense, then they are not going to be treated as integers and should be alphanumeric. A good example of this is a telephone number – adding two telephone numbers together makes no sense at all. Another reason why a telephone number would not be treated as an integer is that in many countries telephone numbers start with 0: this cannot be an integer because integers are not stored with the leading 0. The Form field looks as though it should be treated a bit differently, but the only category we have that it can fit into is alphanumeric.

(b)   Currency/Real – The amount that the student owes for a mountaineering trip that the school is organising.

Date – The date of birth of the student.

Integer – The number of times the student has been absent from school.

Note: You can answer almost anything you want to here as long as the suggestion is sensible.

2   A file is to be set up which will store details of products that a supermarket has in stock.

(a)   Decide what fields should be included in the file, justifying your choices. Clearly indicate which field should be used for the key, explaining why. (6)

(b)   State the data type that would be used for each field, explaining why that data type was chosen. (5)

Summary

❖   Data consists of values that on their own are meaningless; information is data in a context that gives it meaning.

❖   Data is coded to simplify its input and storage by removing any unnecessary detail. It is not done to make the data secret.

❖   Analogue data is physical data and can have any value; digital data is data in regularly defined steps suitable for representation in a computer system.

❖   Verification checks ensure that the data entered was what was meant to be entered. The commonest types are a visual check and double entry.

❖   Validation checks ensure that the data entered is sensible. Common types are range, character and length checks.

❖   An item is a single piece of data, stored in a field. A set of fields that relate to one entity is called a record and is identified by a special field called a key. All related records are stored together as a file.

❖   Records within files can be stored in different ways:

    ◆   serial files have records stored in chronological order;

    ◆   sequential files have records stored in a logical order, normally in order of their key;

    ◆   direct access files have an index that allows access to individual records without reading any intervening ones.

❖   Different types of data are identified so that the computer can store the data in different ways.

5 Hardware, systems and communications

13 Hardware

```
┌─────────────────────────────────────────────────────────────┐
│  Learning objectives                                          │
│                                                               │
│  When you have finished this chapter you will be able to:    │
│                                                               │
│  ❖   describe how different types of computer are distinguished │
│      by their power;                                          │
│                                                               │
│  ❖   recognise a number of different types of input device and │
│      their characteristics, and explain their uses in different │
│      application areas;                                       │
│                                                               │
│  ❖   explain the need to ensure that data stored on a computer │
│      system is in the form that a computer can interpret;    │
│                                                               │
│  ❖   understand that there are different forms of output      │
│      dependent upon the application and that different devices │
│      are needed to produce these different outputs;          │
│                                                               │
│  ❖   distinguish between two different types of storage in a  │
│      computer system: primary and secondary;                 │
│                                                               │
│  ❖   outline different types of storage, their characteristics and uses. │
└─────────────────────────────────────────────────────────────┘
```

13.1 Introduction

IT1a, c

Hardware is a term that means the physical parts of a computer, or 'the bits that are hard', as opposed to the software, which is the instructions that make the computer do something useful.

There are many different types of computers. They are usually categorised by their size and power. Here we are mainly concerned with computers like the ones that you use at school and even smaller ones, such as hand-held computers. However, most processing nowadays is done on very large computers called **mainframe computers** and **supercomputers**. Although they are not a part of our syllabus, you should be aware of why they are important. For example, the calculations needed to do the weather forecast would take so long on a school computer that the day would have ended before we produced the forecast for it. An airline needs a vast database to hold details of seats available on all the flights and a very powerful computer to search it. Customers would have gone to another airline long before one of our computers found the seat they were interested in. These and many other applications need computers that are far more powerful than the ones we are concerned with here.

13.2 Microcomputers and microprocessors

IT1d

The computers that we use are actually called **microcomputers**, to stress that they are different to the really big and powerful computers that we mentioned above. However, all computers, whatever the size, are really in four parts:

➢ Input device – This is used to input data to the computer and tell it what to do. If the computer does not know what to do, it cannot do anything – no matter how powerful it is.

➢ Processor – This is the part that actually does the working out. If there is nothing to work out, you wouldn't need to bother with a computer.

➢ Output device – This lets the computer tell someone what the answers are. It wouldn't be very useful asking a computer to add two numbers if it cannot tell you the answer.

➢ Storage device – This allows files to be stored so they are not lost every time the computer is switched off.

Notice that this list of the different types of hardware matches the diagram of a system in Chapter 1, Figure 1.1.

The processor in a microcomputer consists of a number of different parts. When these parts are small enough, they will all fit on one small silicon chip called a microprocessor. Because the parts are all on one chip, microprocessors are said to be 'integrated'. Microprocessors are designed to carry out one job, normally to control something. Typically a microprocessor will control a video recorder or the timing mechanism in a cooker. But if the one in your video recorder stopped working, you could not take the one out of the cooker and expect it to work the recorder – it will only do one thing. Because of this microprocessors are said to be **dedicated** devices. It is an interesting exercise to see how many devices you can think of that may have a microprocessor in them.

Extension work

We will be looking at different types of computers later. For the moment, keep a look out for references to larger computers and make a note of any that you hear about.

13.3 Input devices

All computers need to be told what to do – there is no point having a powerful computer unless you can make it do something. In order to tell it what to do you have to have a device that lets you input data and commands. This is called an input device. There are almost as many different types of input device as there are applications that computers can be used for. Some of the more common input devices are described below. The important thing to think of when considering an input device is what it needs to input to the computer.

Keyboards

Anyone who has used a computer will be familiar with a keyboard, but how many have studied it? Why are the keys in such a strange order? The standard keyboard is called a 'qwerty' keyboard because that is what is spelt out by the first six letters at the top left of the keyboard. It was designed like that over 100 years ago, long before computers were invented, as that arrangement was the one least likely to result in the machine jamming when typists typed quickly. When electronic keyboards were invented, it became possible to type at any speed without jamming, but everyone was used to the qwerty keyboard and wouldn't change, so for ordinary typing we are stuck with it! There are many other types of keyboard for other purposes, such as an electric piano keyboard, or the keyboard in an ATM (cash machine) outside a bank. These are very different from one another and the keys needed are different. For example, you need a spacebar for typing text, but does the ATM need one? The piano certainly doesn't. If you are asked to describe a keyboard, think about the things that will be input using it – those are the things needed on the keyboard.

Pointing devices

Most computer systems display items on the screen for the user to choose from. The simplest way to do this is by pointing at what you want to choose, and special **touch-sensitive screens** let you use your finger as an input device. You just touch the screen to make your choice. This is wonderful for information screens, such as those at some train stations, because it is virtually weatherproof and vandal proof, but it is no good if I want to choose items on a word processor screen because my finger is too big – I would keep hitting the wrong thing. A better way is to use a pointer on the screen and a device to move it round so that it points at what you want. One **pointing device** with which we are all familiar is the mouse, but there are many others. Again, think of where it will be used and what it is used for. A mouse would be awkward to use with a laptop computer on a bus because of the wire and because there is no flat surface to put it on. So laptops have a tracker ball or a touch pad. A tracker ball is just a mouse turned upside down so that the user can move the ball with their fingers instead of rolling it on a desk, and a touch pad moves the pointer to a new position according to where the finger moves on the pad. Many games consoles use touch pads too. However the pointer is moved, they are basically the same sort of device – move a pointer to choose from a set of options. A special type of pointer is a joystick. This allows the operator to tell the computer which direction to make the pointer move on the screen by moving the stick in the same direction. Many games consoles are controlled by a joystick, but the original and more serious application is to allow a pilot to control an aircraft.

Video digitisers and scanners

Video digitiser is a very complicated name for a very simple idea. In Chapter 12 you looked at the difference between analogue and digital data. What we see around us is in analogue form. If we want to store a picture of what we see in a computer or a microprocessor, then it has to be converted into digital form, using some kind of **analogue to digital converter** (or **A/D converter**). A video digitiser is a device, such as a **scanner**, that turns an analogue picture into a digital one. When an analogue drawing or picture is scanned, it is split into a number of small squares called **pixels**, each one of which is converted into a single colour/shade/brightness that can be stored digitally in the computer's memory. The picture can then be worked on a pixel at a time. The same principle is used in the digital camera.

Remote control

A remote control handset has a number of buttons, each of which means something different. When a button is pressed, a coded signal is sent, normally using an infrared beam, to the device being controlled. When the signal is decoded, the device knows which button has been pressed and what it has to do.

Magnetic input devices

This does not refer to tapes or disks – they are storage devices. Magnetic input comes in two forms: **magnetic stripes** (or sometimes called strips) and **magnetic ink**. Magnetic stripes are often put on the back of credit and bank cards. They contain information about the card holder's account that can be read by a magnetic stripe reader. They are being superseded by small processors embedded in the plastic because these are much harder to copy. Magnetic ink is very specialised. It is the sort of ink used to print account numbers on the bottom of bank cheques. The characters look a little odd to humans but can be read easily enough and because the ink used to print them is magnetic, the characters are easy for computers to read as well, using **magnetic ink character recognition** (**MICR**) software. The only other use for magnetic ink is in passports issued by some countries.

Optical mark readers

Optical mark readers (**OMRs**) are used to detect marks made in pencil on preprinted forms or documents. A computer can then interpret what the mark represents. This is useful when a form is being used to ask people to choose between a few alternatives, for example in multiple-choice exams or on lottery tickets. You may well have to sit a multiple-choice examination in which you have to choose your answer from a list of four or five alternatives. You will probably be asked to mark a line in pencil to show your answer. Using OMR is quick, easy and accurate, though sometimes damaged or creased documents may not be read correctly.

Graphics tablets

A **graphics tablet** is used with a stylus to input freehand work into a computer. The stylus (which could be a pencil if a piece of paper is laid over the tablet) is used to draw whatever you want and the tablet transfers the image to the computer so that it appears on the screen. Graphics tablets are particularly useful for very young or disabled children who are unable to use a keyboard or mouse.

Light pens

A **light pen** is used as a pointing device. The user points the pen at the screen and the computer uses information about the intensity and the timing of the light to highlight the position on the screen that has been pointed at. This can be useful for such things as filling in onscreen data-capture forms.

Microphones

A **microphone** is used for inputting sound to a computer file. Sounds in the natural world are analogue data and, like pictures, they have to be converted into digital data to be stored in the computer. So the sounds are split into tiny parts by the computer, each one of which is given a value. As long as there are enough divisions, the combination sounds the same when played back as it did before it was digitised. (See Figure 13.1.)

Figure 13.1
A digitised sound wave. The wave is split into regular sized 'chunks' of time, each given a distinct value. So an analogue wave has been turned into a series of digits

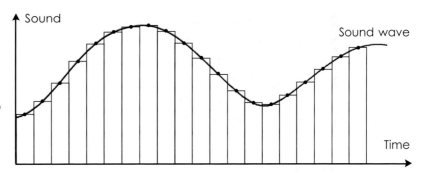

MIDI

Many musical instruments these days are electronic rather than acoustic. Common sense says that if an instrument is electronic and a computer is electronic, then the instrument should be able to communicate with the computer. Unfortunately, this is not normally true and another piece of equipment is needed to go between the computer and the instrument so that the signals from one can be understood by the other. This is called a **MIDI**, which stands for **musical instrument digital interface**. A MIDI is a particular type of serial interface built into a piece of electronic musical equipment so that it can communicate with a computer. Originally there were different standards for communication used by each of the manufacturers, so hardware from different manufacturers could not communicate with each other. In 1983, the major manufacturers agreed a set of codes that would allow their machines to communicate. This set of codes is called the MIDI standard. The codes represent different elements of a musical note, such as volume, pitch, sustain, in binary notation.

Sensors

Sensors are devices that input data automatically from the physical (or real) world. They are roughly divided into two groups. One group measures the sorts of thing that human beings can detect, such as temperature and light. The other group measures the sorts of thing that we cannot detect, such as magnetism or the presence of a microwave beam. The main sensor types are:

➢ temperature   ➢ light

➢ sound   ➢ pressure

➢ magnetism   ➢ touch

➢ radar   ➢ microwave.

The last three are sometimes called proximity sensors when they are used to measure how close the sensor is to something. For example, a radar sensor on a robotic truck will be able to detect the presence of something up ahead of it and thus give a warning that something is 'in close proximity'. Of course, radar can be used for lots of other things besides sensing proximity, such as detecting rainstorms for the weather forecast. Touch sensors tend to be like a switch; for example, if a robot is getting too close to something, a spring-loaded switch will be pressed. This touch sensor is an example of a digital sensor because it is either touching something or it is not. It cannot be half touching. A temperature sensor is an analogue sensor – it can measure 20 °C, or 21 °C, or 20.5 °C, or 20.237 645 … °C. As computers cannot deal with analogue measurements, an A/D converter has to turn these into digital measurements that the computer can use. There is nothing complicated about it, it simply changes readings like 20.237 645 … into something simple like 20.

There are many different types of sensor because every time someone wants to measure something new they invent a new sensor. Imagine that we want to sense whether there is a car next to a traffic light. We could shine a beam of light from one side of the road to a receiver on the other side. Every time a car stops at the lights it will break the beam and a signal will be sent to the computer saying that a car is there (notice this is a digital sensor). Unfortunately, it wouldn't work. Every person who walked across would break the beam too and the computer would have no way of knowing the person wasn't a car. Even a bird sitting on the receiver would be treated as a car! A sound sensor might work if a sign was put up telling the driver to sound the horn, but the people living there wouldn't like it. One type of sensor would work. A magnetic sensor would be able to detect vehicles because they are like very large, weak, magnets, yet it wouldn't notice birds or people, and it would not disturb the local residents – perfect.

Task

Imagine a weather station that is to be set up on the roof of the school. Measurements are to be taken automatically so that a person does not have to keep going onto the roof. Try to think of different sensors that could be used to measure all aspects of the weather.

13.4 Output devices

IT2c, d

As we mentioned before, there is no point in having a computer that can do wonderful things unless it can tell you the results of what it has been doing. This is where we need an output device. There are many types of output device that fall into two categories: those designed to be understood by humans and those that are more automatic.

Monitors/screens

The computer screen or **monitor** is an output device that we are all used to because all microcomputers have one. There are many different types. There are obvious differences, like some are colour and some are monochrome. There are other, more subtle, differences. A screen is made up of a lot of tiny squares called pixels. The quantity of squares on the screen is known as the **resolution** of the screen. The more pixels there are, the higher the resolution and the better the quality of the picture. The picture on the screen is not there permanently like a painting, it actually lasts for a fraction of a second and then has to be produced again by the monitor. This is known as **refreshing** the picture and the time interval between one picture and another is called the refresh rate. It happens so fast that we don't notice it, but if the refresh rate is low the user's eyes can get tired. So people who use systems for long periods of time, such as word processor operators, need monitors with high refresh rates. Some monitors act as input devices as well – such as the touch screen monitors described earlier.

Printers

A printer is a device that produces a hard copy of the output from the computer. It is called a hard copy because you can actually touch it. Unlike a monitor, the output lasts for a long time, as long as you look after the piece of paper. The same sort of measures of quality apply here as they do for the monitor: Is it colour or black and white? How many dots make up the image? However, in this case there is also the question of how the images were made in the first place. There are many different types of printer. The three that you need to consider are:

➤ laser printer

➤ inkjet printer

➤ dot matrix printer.

Laser printers use a laser to produce a positive charge on a sheet of paper and then spray ink powder onto the paper. The ink only sticks where the charge has been left. Lasers produce very high quality images very quickly and are used when it is important to give a good impression of what you are doing, or when there is a large volume of printing to be done. They tend to be expensive to buy, particularly if they are colour printers, though running costs are usually low.

Inkjet printers work by squirting ink at the piece of paper. The quality can be very high, although they are fairly slow because they have to produce the image bit by bit instead of all at once like the laser printer. They are cheap and easily available and consequently they are used with most home computers and in schools and small businesses. Running costs can be high.

Dot matrix printers are different because they have pins that hit an ink ribbon against the paper to produce the printout – the other two types have no parts that actually touch the paper. Dot matrix printers used to be the most common type, but the quality of their output tends to be poor because of the limited number of pins and they are slow. However, they are still used in situations where it is important to produce two copies at the same time, like a carbon copy. This can only be done by the printer physically touching the paper. Examples of this can be found in some supermarkets, where one copy of the receipt is given to the shopper and a second, carbon, copy is kept by the store. Some home computers and schools still use dot matrix printers because they are so cheap to run, but as prices of the other two types come down they are used less and less.

A fourth type of printer is a **plotter**. These work by using pens that are moved around on a sheet of paper, leaving a drawing behind as they go. They are very specialised and are ideal for things like architectural drawings of buildings or wiring diagrams.

Speakers

Speakers are used to produce sound, for instance to accompany a game. Sound makes the game more exciting and hence more desirable. Try playing your favourite game with the sound turned off and notice the difference.

Control devices

The signals produced by a computer are not capable of controlling something like a cooling fan – it needs to send its signals to a special device that can control the fan for it. This special device is called an actuator. There is more about this in the process control part of subsection 14.3 and the extension work that follows it.

Selecting input and output devices

The important questions to ask when you have to choose devices for specific purposes are:

➤ Where will the devices be used? If they are in the street, then they must be weatherproof and not easily damaged, but on an office desk you don't need to be so careful.

➤ What will they be inputting or outputting? Typing a letter is different from taking money out of a cash machine, so you would expect the keyboards you use to look different. You should be able to describe the differences. Similarly, a printer used by students to print out art projects for their IGCSE exams will have to be a colour printer though the text quality will not be too important, while one used by the school office to print letters needs to produce high-quality text but does not have to print in colour. If you were advising the headteacher which printer to buy, you would need to know what it was going to be used for.

➤ Who is going to use it? Many people are not computer literate and have no experience of using computers. There is no point in setting up an information system in a hotel lobby that uses a touch pad or a tracker ball, as many of the people for whom the system is designed will not be able to use it. However, everyone knows how to point, so use a touch screen.

Extension work

A short distance along the road from where I live there is a special school for children with disabilities. Many of these children cannot use the input and output devices that most of us use.

1   What sort of input and output devices could a blind child use when working a computer?

2   What about a child who has no use of their arms?

13.5 Processor power

This is a very difficult section to include in a book because by the time the book is published any figures we put in will be out of date. However, there are 'classes' of computer that you should know about. Be aware while reading this that there can be considerable overlap between the computers in the classes and that there are different ways of categorising them. Starting from the least powerful and working up they are:

➤ Microprocessors – These tend to be embedded in the device that they are controlling, such as a video recorder, and will not work anywhere else.

➤ Microcomputers – These are the computers that you use at school or that you might have at home. They were originally called 'micro' because they were so much lower in power than the standard computer systems used in industry. However, as the size of the components has become smaller, the power of these machines has increased massively.

➤ **Minicomputers** – Typically one of these would be used to control the checkout tills in a supermarket and the access from those tills to the stock database.

➤ Mainframe computers – These are the large-capacity computers used in industry for controlling processes and in offices for maintaining networks and allowing access to shared resources, such as databases.

➤ Supercomputers – These are machines that can do enormous numbers of calculations in a very short time. They are very rare because there are not many applications where such incredible speed is necessary. Typically they are used to produce weather forecasts and for military purposes, such as tracking missiles.

Don't worry about these different types of machine too much. Don't try to learn how fast they are or how much they can store – it would be out of date by the time you took the exam! Just try to remember the different types and the order that they are in. Also, try to have an idea of the sort of places that they would be used.

Extension work

1 Do some research into the power of the different types of computer at the moment. Use computer magazines and the Internet (an interesting site to look at is the one set up by the Cray corporation).

2 Try to find out the whereabouts of the nearest of each of the different computer types. What are they used for?

3 How many different uses can you find for microprocessors in your home and in your school? What sort of input do they need? What processing do they do? What output do they produce?

13.6 Storage media

IT3a–e

There are two types of storage in a computer system:

➤ primary storage

➤ secondary (backing) storage.

Primary storage

The first is the storage inside the computer itself that can be used by the processor. This sort of storage is called the computer's memory. There are two types of memory:

➤ **read-only memory (ROM)**, which stores things permanently and can never be changed;

➤ **random-access memory (RAM)**, which is only usable when the power to the computer is switched on.

ROM is usually very small and only stores the program that the computer needs to switch itself on when the power is turned on. The exception to this is in a microprocessor, which stores the whole program that it uses. For example, the program that runs the timer on a video recorder never changes and is always there when the video is switched on so it is stored on ROM.

RAM stores all the programs and files that the user is using at the moment. When the video recorder is programmed to switch on at 9.00 p.m. and start recording, that information is stored in RAM because tomorrow you may want to change it and record at a different time. If you disconnect the recorder from the electricity supply it will 'forget' that it was supposed to come on at 9.00 p.m. because that information was stored in RAM.

Secondary (backing) storage

When your computer is switched off, all the data stored in RAM is lost. So if you get to the end of a lesson and you are only halfway through doing something, you must save the work onto something else before you turn off or you will lose it. The thing that you save your work on is called secondary storage (or backing storage).

There are several different types of secondary storage that you should know about.

➤ **Magnetic tape** – Tape is cheap and easy to use for storage, but it has one big disadvantage: it is difficult to find something. Imagine you are at the checkout in the supermarket and the assistant scans the barcode on the bottle of water that you are buying. If the stock file is stored on tape, the computer will have to fast forward or rewind to the place on the tape that has the record for bottled water in order to find out the price. Meanwhile you have been chatting to the assistant for five minutes! Tape is an example of a **sequential medium**. The word sequential means that items are stored one after the other in some sort of order (they need to be in order or you wouldn't even be able to fast forward). Tape is rarely used now because there are usually much better alternatives. One of the few things it is still used for is making back-up copies of files. A back-up is a second copy of a file that is kept in a safe place in case something happens to damage the original.

➤ **Magnetic disks** – There are two types: floppy disks and hard disks. In both cases the computer stores material on the disk by magnetising its surface, which is made of a special material. A computer can then read information back from the disk by examining the pattern of magnetisation. Because the surface is a flat disk and not a long tape, the information from anywhere on the disk can be read almost straightaway – this is much quicker than finding information on a tape. Floppy disks are made of plastic similar to the plastic used to make a tape. Hard disks are made of metal. Floppy disks are stored outside the computer case and are useful for moving data from one computer to another, perhaps because you want to take a piece of work home or because you want to post it to someone because it is too confidential to risk sending as an email attachment. Hard disks normally stay inside the computer box because they are very easily damaged. Nowadays they can store enormous amounts of data, but the first that we used in my school, twenty years ago, was only 18 Mbyte, and we thought that was massive. Nowadays the hard drive stores all the software and data files that are used on the computer. Imagine that crashing and everything being lost: it would be a nightmare. That is why most people make the back-up copies we mentioned before, although nowadays they would probably use a CD-ROM to store it on.

➤ CD-ROM – The data is still stored on a medium in the shape of a disk. The difference is that this is written onto and read from using the light from a laser instead of magnetism. For this reason it is known as an **optical disk**. Be careful about how you describe these. Once they have had data put on them they cannot be written onto again – that is why they are called ROM, which stands for read-only memory). They are used particularly for importing software to a computer system.

➤ CD-Rewritable – These are very similar to CD-ROMs, except that it is possible to put new information on them. This requires a special drive that allows more information to be written (or 'burned') onto the surface. This a destructive process, which means that eventually the disk will be used up and have to be replaced. The big advantage over floppy disks is that they store far more data, yet they are still fully portable, unlike most hard disks. These CDs are used whenever large quantities of data need to be stored and remain portable. A particular use is for storing back-up files.

Extension work

It is easy for a computer to work out where it is on a magnetic tape because it can measure how far it has wound through it. Put simply, if it knows that information on bottled water is 874 units (could be centimetres or inches, or even a special unit that only the computer uses) from the start of the tape, it can find it again by starting at the beginning of the tape and measuring 874 units along.

1   Find out how it can do this without having to start from the beginning of the tape every time it wants to find some information.

2   How does it remember not only that bottled water is 874 units along the tape, but also where all the other things are?

It is not so easy for the computer to do this using a disk. The disk has a large amount of data on it and the computer can only find the correct data if it knows whereabouts it is on the surface. It does this by splitting the surface into many small areas called blocks. Then, if the computer knows that bottled water is in block C21, it can go straight there.

This process of splitting the disk up into small areas is called **formatting** (see Figure 13.2) and is done by the operating system (see Chapter 14).

3   The index is in the middle track. Why do you think this is?

4   If you are formatting a disk, why do you have to be very careful?

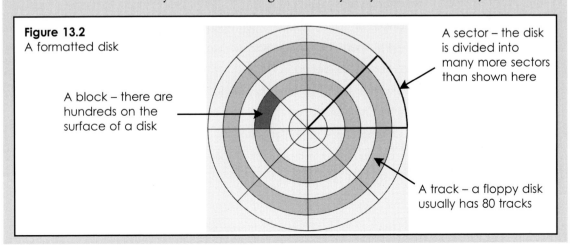

Figure 13.2
A formatted disk

A block – there are hundreds on the surface of a disk

A sector – the disk is divided into many more sectors than shown here

A track – a floppy disk usually has 80 tracks

Example questions

1   A computer is used to control the traffic at a busy road junction. It is also necessary to provide a pedestrian crossing so that pedestrians can cross the road safely.

(a)   State what input devices could be used and the reason they are necessary.   (4)

(b)   Explain what devices the system would need to control.   (3)

(c)   Describe the processing that the computer would need to carry out in order to make acceptable decisions.   (6)

Suggested answers

(a)   ◆ Something to measure the presence of a vehicle / on each street, such as: radar / infrared / microwave / induction loop in the road.

◆ Something to tell the system the lengths of the queues of traffic, using the same sensors as above but placed at a distance from the lights.

◆ Some means by which the pedestrian can tell the system they are waiting, such as a button to press.

◆ Some means to tell the processor whether a pedestrian is still crossing the road, such as: radar / infrared / microwave.

(b)   ◆ The lights, in order to control the vehicles.

◆ Pedestrian lights to indicate whether it is safe to cross.

◆ Sound (such as a beeper) to indicate safety for a blind pedestrian.

(c)   ◆ Allow time for cars to pass in one direction. This would be based on the messages from the sensors informing the system about the length of queue.

◆ Change those lights to red.

◆ Check on status of pedestrian button:

– if pushed, then set pedestrian lights green;

– wait for set period.

◆ Check crossing for presence of pedestrians.

◆ When no pedestrians:

– change pedestrian lights to red;

– change other vehicle lights to green.

◆ Repeat instructions.

Notes: Notice that there are plenty of possible answers for the sensors and the things that need to be controlled by the system. The important thing here is not so much getting the correct answers, there are no single correct answers, as getting answers that are sensible. As we said in the text, a light sensor would not be sensible, but if you can give a good reason for a different sensor you will get the marks. Notice also that the reasons are just as important as the sensors themselves. In part (b), notice that the question said 'system', not 'computer'. There is a big difference. If the question had said 'computer', then your answer could have been simply 'it controls actuators'. But this question says 'system' and the actuators are part of the system, so your answer has to list the devices that come after the actuators. Part (c) has lots of answers. Notice that the question asks for a description of the processing, not an algorithm, and certainly not pseudocode. It does not mean that you would lose marks if you answered in the form of an algorithm, but it is not needed.

2   An automatic washing machine is controlled by a microprocessor.

(a)   Explain how a microprocessor differs from a microcomputer.   (2)

(b)   Explain why a sensor is needed to tell the microprocessor whether the door is shut.   (2)

(c)   Describe the processing necessary to ensure that the floor does not get flooded when the washing machine is turned on.   (4)

(d)   State two other sensors that could be used in a microprocessor-controlled washing machine, explaining why they are necessary.   (4)

(e)   Explain why an actuator is needed in this control system and state one thing that it would need to control.   (3)

3(a)   State two tasks that can be done by robots in a car factory.   (2)

(b)   Explain why these tasks are particularly suited to being done by robots rather than humans.   (3)

(c)   Describe how a microprocessor-controlled robot truck can move around a factory safely. Your answer should include details of input to the system, processing that is necessary and output to move the robot truck.   (6)

4   Describe a suitable set of hardware for an information system that is going to be standing on the platform of a railway station to give passengers information about train times.   (6)

5   A student at a school uses the school network of computers during a lesson in order to start writing an essay. The student takes the half-finished essay home so that she can continue to work on it that night. When the students have left school, the technician has

to load a new piece of software onto the school system and then make a back-up of all the students' work.

Describe the different storage media that are being used by the student and the technician, giving reasons why they are used. (8)

6   Explain the differences between the keyboard used to type in a history essay and the one used at an ATM to take money out of your bank account. (6)

Summary

❖   Microcomputers are the type of computer common to school and home, but there are many other, larger, machines that are in use in the world. When the components of a computer are so small that they all fit on one chip, it is called a microprocessor.

❖   Input devices include keyboards, pointers and graphics devices, magnetic input by stripes and ink, microphones for sound and sensors to measure values from the physical world.

❖   Analogue to digital converters and MIDI devices change data from the form in which it is collected to a form that can be used by the computer.

❖   Output devices include monitors, printers, speakers and actuators.

❖   There are two types of storage: primary and secondary. Primary storage is inside the computer and is of two types: ROM and RAM. Secondary storage is user-controlled, and is more permanent than RAM – something is erased only when the user wants to erase it. It may be in the computer box or external.

❖   Storage devices include magnetic tape, magnetic disks and optical disks. Each type has different characteristics and is used for different purposes.

14 | Systems and communications

Learning objectives

When you have finished this chapter you will be able to:

❖ explain the need for an operating system;

❖ distinguish between some of the many types of operating system and describe the characteristics and uses of some;

❖ describe how the operating system controls communication between the computer and external entities, both machine and human;

❖ state how the operating system controls the storage of data on both memory and external storage devices;

❖ explain why communication is necessary between the computer and external devices and how this communication is controlled.

14.1 Operating system facilities

Chapter 11 described the meaning of software as 'programs, routines and procedures (together with their associated documentation) that can be run on a computer system'. We mentioned at the start of that chapter that there are two types of software necessary to make a computer do something useful: applications software and operating system software.

Applications software is written so that a computer system can do something that would have to be done even if computers did not exist. For example, I am sitting at a computer keyboard writing this book. If I did not have a computer, I would be using a typewriter. The word processing software allows me to use the computer in the same way that I would use a typewriter.

It is the second type of software, operating system software, that we are going to study in this chapter. The operating system is a program (or, more likely, a set of programs) that controls the operation of the computer.

However much a computer cost, however great the specification, without an operating system it is only a useless lump of plastic and metal. It would make a very expensive paperweight! Just as my computer needs a word processing program to tell it what to do when I hit a particular key on the keyboard, the computer needs a program to tell it what to do to start itself up in the morning, how to send messages to the screen, how to talk to the printer, and lots of other things that don't concern me when I am typing at my keyboard. Programs that tell the computer how to do these things are called the operating system. If you think of the operating system as the set of programs that allow the computer to 'live', you won't go far wrong.

Don't be put off by the different names for the operating system. It can be called:

➢ the operating system (or OS)

➢ operating system software

➢ system software.

These all mean the same thing.

14.2 The need for an operating system

When computers were first invented, there were no operating systems. This meant that if you wanted to make the computer add two numbers together, you not only had to tell it the two numbers, you also had to tell it where the two numbers were, how to do the sum and how to output the answer.

This was a very unsatisfactory state of affairs – not only did even the simplest of things take a long time to do, but also the people who used the computers had to be scientists who understood how they worked.

Soon, people started to write sets of instructions (programs) to tell the computer how to do some of the more common things that it needed to do. This meant that the people who wanted to use them could concentrate on solving their problem instead of having to tell the computer what to do. These programs were the very first operating systems.

A car is a complex machine that people find very useful, just like a computer. But, just like a computer, it won't work unless it is told what to do. The driver tells the car how to behave, in much the same way as an operating system tells a computer how to behave. If I were to drive a sports car, I would probably drive very slowly and carefully, while a racing driver would drive it very quickly, and would be able to take corners at much higher speeds. Just as the same car can act very differently depending on who is driving it, so the same computer will work very differently depending on which operating system is being used.

The next section introduces some of the different ways that the computer can be made to work by having different operating systems loaded into it.

14.3 Examples of different operating systems

IT4d, e, g;
7.1d

These are just some of the types of operating system (OS) available.

Batch OS

Imagine a factory in which each of the workers has to input an ID number when they come to work and again when they have to leave. The computer can work out their pay at the end of the week because it knows how long they have been at work. At the end of the week the computer is going to be very busy working out the pay, but it cannot do that until the last worker has left the factory at the end of the week. Until then it might as well be used for other things. It would be silly to stop the computer every time someone wanted to start work or leave, so all these pieces of information are stored up in one large batch and used when the computer isn't doing anything else. (See Figure 14.1.)

Figure 14.1
Batch processing

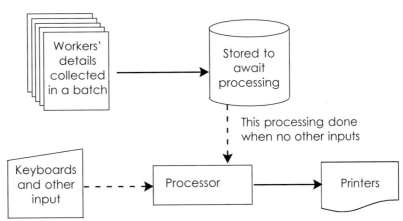

The keyboard is used during office hours and is then disconnected to allow the processor to concentrate on the batched data

Real-time OS (real-time transaction processing)

Imagine playing a computer game in which the object is to drive a racing car around a track. If there is a right-hand bend, then the player needs to send a signal to the computer to turn right. The computer needs to turn right straightaway or the car will crash. When an application needs to be dealt with immediately, it is a real-time application.

Online and offline OS

These are very simple concepts. If the input device is connected to the computer and input is sent to the computer for immediate processing, this is called online. When the input is saved and sent to the computer later, this is called offline. Online and offline processing are illustrated in Figure 14.2.

Figure 14.2
(a) Online processing – input made by the user is sent direct to the processor for immediate action

(b) Offline processing – input made by the user is sent to a storage device and only sent to the processor after all the input is done

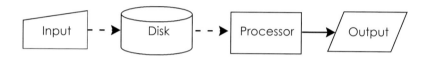

Real-time applications are said to be online applications, while batch processing is carried out offline because the input is collected first.

Multi-access OS

This allows more than one person to use the same computer at the same time. A good example is when you and a friend decide to race each other on a computer racing game. It works because the computer is much faster at doing things than we are, so it can check what you want to be done to your car and then check your friend's car, and then go back to yours, so quickly that each of you feels as if you are the only one using the machine. Figure 14.3 shows a larger multi-access system in which each terminal is given some time on the processor before it moves on to the next person. The processor is so fast that each person thinks they are online all the time.

Figure 14.3
A multi-access system

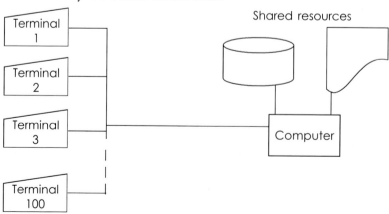

Network OS

Most people think that networks are examples of multi-access operating systems because they allow access to more than one person at a time. There is a big difference. A multi-access system has only one computer – there may be lots of keyboards and screens, but only one computer. In a network, each workstation has its own computer. The computers are connected up so that they can share printers and hard disk drives, they can share all the programs on the system and people can access their work from any computer on the network. However, when the software is loaded up, the computer can be disconnected from the network and will work like your computer at home (until it needs a printer).

As we mentioned in the extension work in Chapter 1, there are two different sorts of network. A network in which the computers are close together and connected with wires is called a local area network (LAN). A network in which the computers are a long way apart is called a wide area network (WAN). Most of us use both sorts: your school system is probably a LAN and the Internet is a WAN. A way of telling the difference is that all the computers in a WAN need modems, or something similar, to allow them to communicate – they are too far apart to be connected directly by wires. Figure 14.4 shows a typical LAN.

Figure 14.4
A typical LAN. Other arrangements are possible – for instance, the network doesn't have to have a server

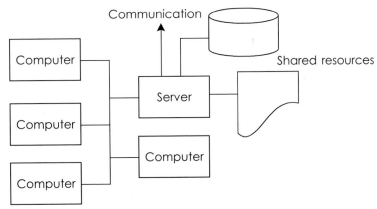

A big advantage of a network is that it makes it possible to share hardware. You are probably used to sharing a printer at school – it is a bit annoying having to wait when lots of people want a printout, but it is also very cheap because a network only needs one printer. The same is true of software. And it is useful not having to sit at the same machine every time you come to the computer room – as the machines are all connected up it is possible to sit anywhere. One big problem, though, is stopping other people looking at your work, which is why we need to take care that our data files are kept private, as discussed in Chapter 2. Most systems have **user IDs** and passwords. The user

ID is necessary so that the system knows who you are and which files it should let you see, the password is so that you can assure the computer that you are who you say you are.

Multitasking OS

This is exactly what it says. When you sit at your computer, you might have a word processor on the screen that you are using to type up an essay. You decide that it would be good to include a table from a spreadsheet, so you cut and paste it in. You may be connected to your email provider so that any new messages appear immediately on the screen. While all this is going on, you may be listening to music from a CD. Your computer is managing to carry out lots of tasks at the same time – it is multitasking.

Process control OS

This is the automatic monitoring and control of a machine in industry. Sensors (see Chapter 13) are used to provide the computer with information about what the machine is doing and then decisions are made by the computer about what the machine should do next.

Extension work

Batch operating systems were the first to be developed. They were invented to stop people slowing the computer down. They can do this because the person is no longer connected to the machine (they are offline systems). Batch systems are run when the computer is not needed for anything else, often at night when the workers have gone home. Banks print their customers' bank statements at night and then in the morning change the operating system of the computer to multi-access so that other work can be done.

Multi-access systems work on a principle called time sharing. The computer gives the first person using the system a little bit of time (called a time slice) and then saves their work and goes on to the next person. This continues until all the people on the system have had a time slice, then the first person is given control again. The system works because computers operate so quickly. Each person is probably only being given 1/100th of a second of computer time, but the computer comes back to them so quickly that they think they are the only one using the machine. A good example of a multi-access system is the supermarket checkout system in which all the tills are connected to one computer. It works so quickly that the workers and shoppers do not notice any delay.

LAN networks are categorised as one of three different types, depending on the pattern of the wiring connecting the computers together:

➢ a bus network, in which the computers are connected in a line;

➢ a ring network, which is a bus network with the two ends joined up;

➢ a star network, in which all the computers are connected separately to the hub or server.

These are illustrated in Figure 14.5.

Figure 14.5
Three different types of network

Computers

Some resources spread around the system

(a) A bus network

Terminators at end of the bus

Server

Shared resources

(b) A ring network

Server

(c) A star network

Server

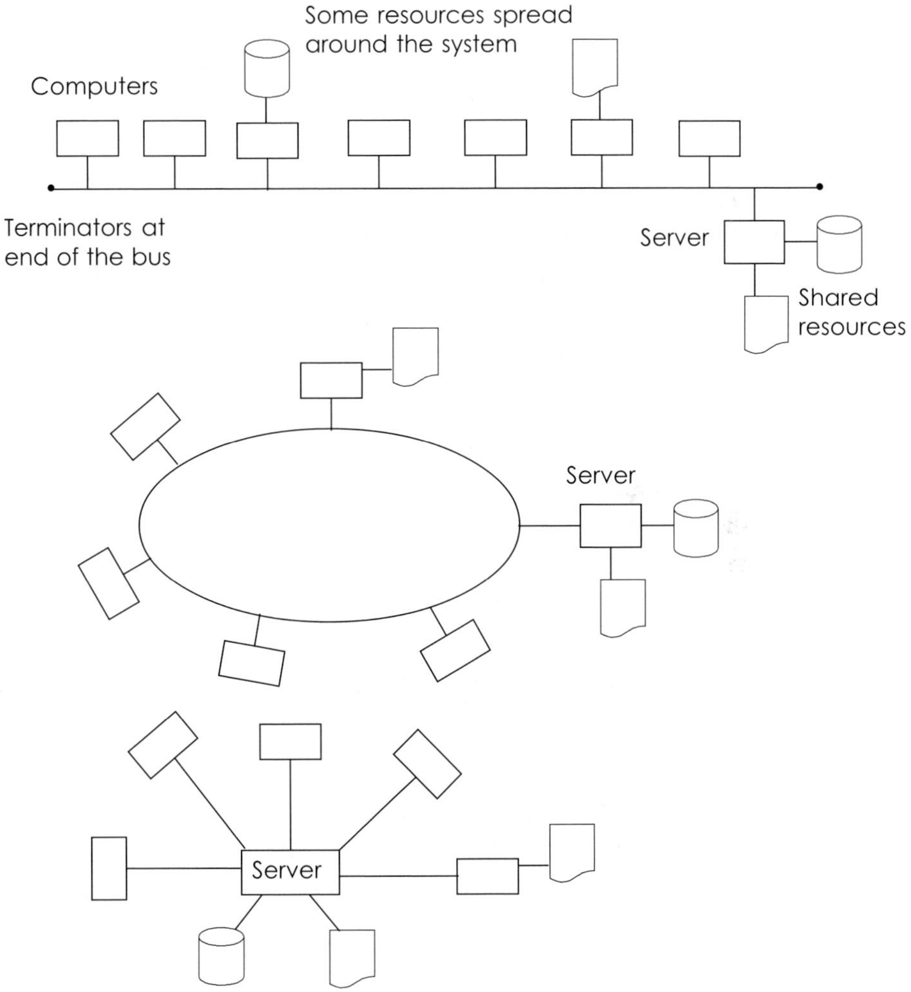

As the pattern (known as a topology) gets more complex, the wiring becomes harder to achieve and more expensive to produce, but conversely it becomes more reliable and messages are transmitted more quickly.

Other connection methods can be used in networks. LANs can be connected using radio, lasers or microwaves. WANs can use ISDN or broadband cables. However, the basic principles stated above remain true.

Most computer users use a **graphical user interface** (GUI – see subsection 14.4) for multitasking. These are sometimes called WIMPs, which stands for windows, **icons**, menus, pointer. There is more about this in subsection 14.4, but note here that these **interfaces** use windows. The user can have lots of windows on the screen at the same time, as shown in Figure 14.6, each doing something different – a perfect example of a multitasking environment.

Figure 14.6
A screenshot showing a multitasking environment

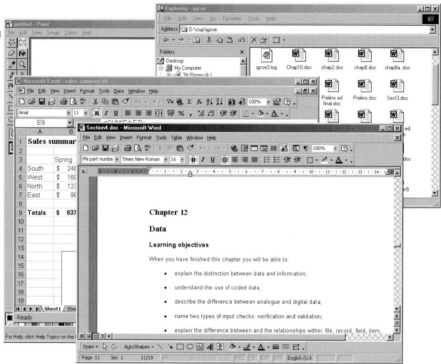

The basic steps of process control – sense/process/action – were described earlier, but it is important to go a little further. Often, the measurement taken by the sensor will be in analogue form and will need to be changed into digital form by a converter (see Chapter 12). An input not mentioned above is the one from the operator who sets the values that the computer needs to maintain. These are known as the parameters. The majority of the processing in process control is done to maintain these parameters. After the decision has been made, the computer has to take some action automatically. Unfortunately, the computer does not produce a signal strong enough to control a physical device, so it needs an actuator. This accepts the signal from the computer and is able to alter the physical device that is being controlled. One last thing: imagine a system that controls the temperature in a chemical reaction. The computer will receive a signal from the thermistor (see Chapter 13) and compare it with the parameters that it has been given. A decision is then made as to whether to increase the temperature or not. When the second reading is sent from the sensor, the computer compares it with the parameters, but it can also compare it with the previous temperature that was measured. This time it not only works out whether the temperature needs changing, but it can also see whether the decision that it made last time has had any effect. This comparison with an earlier measurement is known as feedback. Figure 14.7 shows a simple illustration of process control.

Figure 14.7
Process control

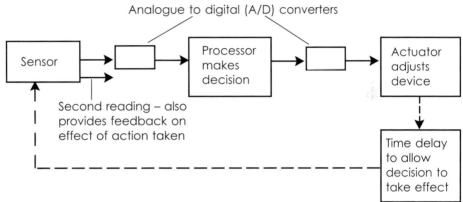

14.4 Interfaces

If you want to use a computer, you have to be able to talk to it and it has to be able to give you the answer to what you want it to do. To do this we use a **human/computer interface** or **HCI**. There is nothing complicated about this: an HCI is simply where the human and the computer have got together to communicate. There are many different types of HCI. You have to know about two of them:

➢ graphical user interface (GUI);

➢ **command-based interface**.

The graphical user interface (also known as a WIMP interface), which you met earlier in this chapter, is the sort of interface that most modern computers offer the user. It is doubtless the sort that you have on your home computer and that you use on the school computers. It is called 'graphical' because it makes use of icons (graphics) to stand for things. This makes it is easy for us to understand and makes the computer seem more user-friendly. GUIs are useful to managers of computer systems because they allow the manager to easily restrict access to the different areas of the system.

A command-based interface is far more difficult to use because the user has to type in what they want the computer to do. This means they have to:

➢ know what the commands are;

➢ type them in the correct order;

➢ be very careful what they are typing;

➢ understand a little of how the computer system works.

However, a command-based interface can be very useful for someone like a network manager because it gives them access to any part of the system very quickly.

14.5 The use of file directories

It does not take long to fill a computer system with lots of data. Each set of data, whether it is something you have typed in, a piece of software or part of the operating system, is called a file. Very soon there are hundreds of files on the system and they need sorting out so they can be found again. Operating systems give the user a number of ways to look after their files. These are simply little programs designed to help look after the files. They include:

➢ Copy – This allows the user to copy files, or parts of files, from one place to another. This is very useful if you want to make a copy of a file in case the original gets damaged in some way.

➢ Move – Sometimes a file may end up being stored in the wrong place. The Move program allows the user to move the file to where it should be stored.

➢ List – This searches through the different files to find all those of the same type. For instance, it may find all those created in July, or all those created on the word processor. Having found them, it will report the list of files found, probably by printing the file names out.

➢ Print – This is an easy one! This is a little program that tells the computer how to print out the chosen files.

The files are stored on some type of backing storage. The system keeps a check on them by storing details of each file in a **file directory**. This is just like the index of a book and it is used in the same way. It allows the system to find files more easily. Sometimes it is useful to lump some files together – for instance, I may want to store all the files about this book separately from the other files that I store. This sort of index of files of a particular type is called a **subdirectory**.

All the little programs that have been mentioned here are part of the operating system. Their job is to make things easier for the user of the system. There are a lot more of them, but that is enough for this syllabus.

14.6 How the processor communicates with its peripherals

A computer consists of more than just the processor. Input devices such as keyboards and sensors have to be communicated with, as do output and storage devices. A problem can arise: which part starts off the communication? Think of the processor in a computer system as being the all-powerful part. It can start talking to any of the other parts whenever it wants to, but if something like a printer wants to talk to the processor it needs to get the processor's attention and also its permission. The way that it does this is to send an **interrupt** signal asking the processor to stop what it is doing and do something else. It is called this because it is asking the processor to interrupt what is being processed at the moment. The processor receives the interrupt and decides how important it is. If it is very important, it stops what it is doing and deals with it immediately; but if not, it puts it in a queue with all the other interrupts that need to be dealt with. Whereabouts it goes in the queue depends on how important it is. This importance is called its **priority**.

Imagine a robot car moving across a floor. It has lots of sensors of different types telling the processor what is around it, where it is, how fast it is going and so on. If a sensor spots an obstruction in front of it, it must tell the processor. It sends an interrupt that has a high priority because it must be dealt with quickly or the car will hit the obstruction. Another way of dealing with the problem is for the processor to ask each of the sensors in turn whether they have anything to report. Notice that in this system the processor is in command. The sensors only send data when they are told to. The processor works so quickly that there is little chance of the car hitting the obstruction before the processor gets to that sensor. When the processor is in command like this, it is known as a **polling** system.

Extension work

When a computer wants to send a file to a printer to be printed out, it first needs to establish contact with the printer. It needs to make sure it is switched on, that it is ready to receive data, that it has enough paper and ink, and so on. These first signals are called **handshaking**. The processor then sends the first character and the printer prints it, then it sends the second character, and so on. This is a terrible waste of time for the processor because it can work far faster than this. The problem is created because the system is working at the speed of the slowest part (the printer). A solution is for the processor to send the file to a special area of storage called a **buffer** and then let that send the characters to the printer while the processor gets on with something else. Unfortunately, the processor won't spot if a problem arises (perhaps the printer runs out of paper) or if the printer uses up all the data in the buffer and wants some more, because it is doing other things. So the printer can send an interrupt saying 'give me more paper', or 'put some more in the buffer'.

When the data is being sent from one place to another, there is a danger that it won't arrive safely. As mentioned earlier, all data in a computer system is stored as numbers – each letter of the alphabet has a code number. Before a set of characters is sent from one place to another, the computer adds all the numbers up. When the characters get to where they are going, they are added up again. If the two answers don't match, then a mistake has been made in sending the numbers. This special sum that is done to check that the data has reached its destination correctly is known as a **checksum**.

Example questions

1   Describe what is meant by system software.   (2)

Suggested answers

◆   System software controls how the computer system works.

◆   It comprises a series of programs.

◆   Each of these programs makes the computer able to carry out a standard task.

Notes: Always look at the first word of the question and the number of marks available. Here it says 'describe'. This means your answer needs to include a bit more than just a fact. It means say something and then add something. Also, the two marks at the end of the question are very important. If there are two marks and you have said only one thing, you can have only one mark, however well you have said your one thing.

There are three points in the mark scheme that the examiner will accept – one for each of the lines in our answer – even though there are only two marks available. As mentioned earlier, it is quite common for there to be more mark points than marks available because it would be unfair to expect you to come up with the full answer in the exam.

All the answers here are in the chapter that you have just looked at. This is known as a 'book work' type of question, because if you learn what you read in the book, you should be able to answer the question, even if you don't understand it. Some of the questions on the paper will be like this because the examiner has to test whether or not you have studied the course. Some of the questions will be such that you have to show that you have understood what you have learned and can apply it. The next question is a mixture of the two types.

2(a)   Explain what is meant by each of the following terms:

(i) batch processing

(ii) real-time processing

(iii) online processing

(iv) offline processing.   (4)

(b)   A computer game requires the user to drive a car around a race track.

Choose two of the terms in part (a) that would be used to describe the type of processing required, justifying your answer.   (3)

Suggested answers

(a)   (i) Inputs are collected together. They are processed later.

(ii) Processing is carried out immediately. Processing is carried out quickly enough to affect the next input.

(iii) The input device is connected to the computer.

(iv) The input device is not connected to the computer.

(b)   Real-time processing – in order to move the car quickly enough real-time processing must be used. Real-time is the only type of processing that can be done quickly enough to affect the next input.

Online processing – the input device must be connected to the computer or the inputs will not get there.

Notes: Not all the parts of the question have more than one mark point that can be made. Examiners try to have more than one mark point in the scheme for each mark, but it is not always possible. The only thing you can say about online processing is that the input device is connected to the computer, what other mark point can there be?

Part (b) is different. You have told the examiner that you know about the four things asked for; in part (b) you are demonstrating that you understand how they are used. This is not just a case of remembering and is considered to be very much more difficult. All papers, and many questions, have a mixture of the two types.

3   A burglar alarm system has a number of sensors connected to a processor. The system can work either by using an interrupt system or a polling system.

(a)   Describe how this system could use

(i) polling   (2)

(ii) interrupts   (2)

to create an effective burglar alarm.

(b)   State which of these systems would be the most effective, giving a reason for your answer.   (1)

Suggested answers

(a)   (i) Each sensor is contacted by the processor.

Each sensor is contacted in turn, some may be contacted more often, depending on importance.

The sensor then returns a message stating whether or not there is a change.

(ii) The processor can get on with other tasks.

The sensors only communicate when they need to. They communicate by interrupt (high priority).

(b)   *Either*

Polling, because this means that if a burglar cuts a wire, then the system knows that something is wrong.

Or

Interrupts, because then the computer can be used for other things while running the burglar alarm in the background.

Notes: The reasoning here is slightly astray because the computer could probably run a polling system and allow for other tasks to be done. However, it would depend on the size of the alarm system (the security system in a power station close to where I live is a polling system with 96,000 sensors) and the types of other applications being run. Notice also that there is no mark for the type of system in (b) because either could be considered reasonable. The mark is for the reason.

4   Describe a directory system in a windows-based interface. You should explain the terms: 'root directory', 'subdirectory' and 'file' in your answer.   (6)

Summary

❖   Operating systems are distinct software whose task is to control the hardware and to provide a user interface.

❖   Different types of operating system include: batch, online, multi-access, real-time, multitasking, network and process control.

❖   Different types of interface controlled by the operating system include command-based and GUI interfaces.

❖   Operating systems use small programs to control files. These include: copy, move, list and print. Details of each file are stored in a file directory.

❖   Methods of communication between the computer and its external devices include the use of: buffers, interrupts, priorities and handshaking.

15 | Types of system

15.1 Introduction

All computer systems are basically the same. They have something that will give them data, which is then processed in some way and then the results are output from the system. Although all systems have this in common, different systems can be used in different ways. Sometimes the difference can be seen because of particular pieces of hardware used – for instance, a system that uses sensors is going to be a control system of some sort. But the biggest difference is one that you don't see until the systems are switched on. This is because it is a difference in the software used to control the system. We met the idea of an operating system in Chapter 14, and we will now give a few extra ideas about each one. It is probably a good idea to treat this chapter as extension work, because the basic principles of the different types of operating systems have been discussed earlier. For each of the systems described in this chapter, refer back to Chapter 1 and decide which of the applications mentioned it would be appropriate for.

15.2 Batch processing

The important phrase concerned with batch processing is 'time dependency'. If you are playing a driving game, then you expect that when you turn the steering wheel, the screen image of your car will turn immediately. It would be a very difficult game if you had to wait 10 minutes for your car to turn. The processing that the computer needs to do is **time dependent** because it must be done in a reasonable amount of time for that application or it might as well not bother. If you are at the checkout in the supermarket, you expect the till to find the price of each item immediately. If the assistant scanned in the barcode of an item and then told you that you would have to wait until Friday to find out how much it cost, you would go to the supermarket next door. However, if you turn the light on and then do some cooking, you don't expect a bill to be produced immediately for the use of the light and then another one for turning on the cooker. You expect all the records of the electricity you have used to be stored until there is enough to make it worthwhile sending you a bill. This is batching. Batch processing has the following characteristics:

➤ the output is not time dependent;

➤ there is a large amount of data, otherwise it is not worth setting up a special operating system for;

➤ the batch of data is processed in one go while the computer is not being used for anything else;

➤ there should be no interruptions from an operator;

➤ the processing is controlled from the programming with very little need of human control; this means that the processing is usually quite simple and that the processing is normally the same from one set of data to the next.

The electricity bill is a very good example. It is not the sort of output that has to be produced to a tight time schedule and the amount of data is enormous because every house in the country has to receive a bill. The computer system at the electricity company is probably not doing anything at night when the offices are shut, so it can be used for this. Also, there is probably no one around because the workers have gone home, so it won't be interrupted by human beings. The processing is very simple and always the same, it just calculates the bill and prints it out, so the program should be easy to write.

15.3 Single-user and multi-access systems

A single-user system is a computer system like the one you may have at home, where only one person can use the processor at a time. It is sometimes called a personal computer (PC) and sometimes a stand-alone machine, because it does not have to be connected to another one. The typical operating system can be called a multitasking system because it appears to do several things at once. Notice that an 'online' system simply means that the user is connected to the processor.

Multi-access systems use a single processor to which many people have access at what seems to them to be the same time. The method was described in Chapter 14, and there is little to add except that the process of going from one machine to another is called a 'round robin', and a way of speeding the system up is to miss out machines that have nothing else that they want to do. If one of the workstations is turned off, then obviously it is a waste of time the processor giving it some time because it won't need anything. Even if the person who is using a workstation is thinking, again it would be silly holding the rest of the workstations up. So a signal is sent to the processor from all machines that need time and the processor does not bother with any machine that has not sent a signal. These signals are called flags.

Multi-access systems are used when very little processing power is needed at the workstations so that one central processor can handle it all. A good example is an information system in a train station. There may be a workstation on each platform that passengers can use to ask about train times. There is very little work for the processor to do and each one will only be used for short periods of time. Another distinct advantage of using a multi-access system in this example is that only one copy of the train timetable needs to be stored, so if a train time is changed, it only has to be changed once instead of at each machine. In this example none of the workstations would need to do any processing because it is done centrally. Workstations like this are known as **dumb terminals**. Sometimes, for instance in a supermarket checkout system, it is important for the workstations to do some of their own work (like doing a validation check on the barcodes that have been read. These are called **smart terminals** but they would not compare with a personal computer.

15.4 Network systems

Again, most of this work is in Chapter 14. It is very important to remember that a system is only a network if it consists of individual computers that are joined together. Sometimes the difference between a multi-access system and a network is very small; it all depends on how 'intelligent' the workstations are. In Chapter 14 we said that a network was a set of computers that were joined together to share resources such as printers and software. That is true, but far more important is the sharing of files of data. These files are the reason why the network was set up in the first place.

It is not unusual to split the files up around the network. If you have a network in your school, it may well be that the software is stored on the hard disk of one machine while the lower school work is stored on another and the upper school project work is stored on another. In this way the important items have been split up around the network – this is a **distributed network**. The users don't know anything about this and don't have to do anything special to get what they want; the operating system does everything for them. However, there are two very important effects of having a distributed network. The first is that when the information is spread around the network, communications are speeded up because requests are not all going through the same place. The second is that security is improved because, for instance, it is easier to make sure that the lower school students cannot get access to the machine that stores the upper school project work. Another way of protecting your project would be to store it somewhere that is not on the network. If you keep a floppy disk in your bag and store your work on that, then nobody can damage it. If you do this, you are using shared resources to store the software you use (that is, on the network) while you are using the local resource of the machine's floppy disk drive to load up your project.

15.5 Control systems and automated systems

IT7.1d

Most of this work has already been covered in Chapter 14. One important extra point is that the system needs to be provided with two pieces of information about timing. The first is how long the system will operate for. If the system is automatically storing the temperature of an experiment in your science laboratory, then it is probably not sensible to make the system record the temperature for a matter of days if the experiment only lasted half an hour. But if the system is recording temperatures of the earth's surface to measure differences between the seasons, then it must continue for a year or more. A simpler example is a computer-controlled air-conditioning system in an office block. Does it need to be on all night? The second piece of timing information that the system needs is how often to take readings from the sensor. If the sensor is measuring the heat in a nuclear reactor so that the system can control the temperature, it will need to be very done at short time intervals, whereas a home heating system must not take the readings too often. Enough time must be left to ensure that the previous decision has taken effect, otherwise feedback from the system cannot be used.

Although a control system is a type of automated system, it is possible to have an automated system that is not a control system. For example, an automatic weather station that simply collects data without making any attempt to use it to control its environment is an automated system without being a control system.

Some systems are **closed systems** that have little contact with the outside world and will only control a small part of it. Such systems are called dedicated systems because they do only one thing, or **embedded systems** because they are inside the items that they control. You met these in Chapter 14.

15.6 Multimedia systems

The first question that needs to be answered is 'What is meant by multimedia?' A medium in this context is a means of conveying information, so a multimedia system is one that uses lots of different ways to communicate information. There are many different media that human beings can recognise and that could be used by a computer for output, for example:

➢ music or other sounds can be produced through speakers;

➢ graphics and text can be printed out, displayed on a monitor or output to a projector so that large audiences can see it;

➢ touch can be simulated so that the user can take part in a **virtual reality** world using specially designed headgear and gloves.

All of these are different media, so if a computer produces more than one at a time, it is being used as a multimedia computer system. Strictly speaking, that would include a system that produced a page of text with a picture in it. Nowadays, we would probably expect something a little bit more spectacular than that, but if your computer will allow you to do a bit of animation while playing some music, then it is a multimedia computer.

Notice the difference between the system that will produce text with a picture and the one that produces animation and music – the second one is time sensitive. If there is a delay of a couple of seconds in producing a page of text and picture, it doesn't matter, whereas a similar delay during an animation or playing a tune will make the output look or sound silly. This means that, historically, only powerful and expensive machines could cope with being multimedia machines because they needed very fast processors. Nowadays, any PC that you buy is powerful enough.

Summary

❖ This chapter has expanded on the work in Chapter 14 on different operating systems to include more detailed examples of their use.

6 Coursework project and practical work

Chapters 16 to 22 are written specifically for GCE O Level and IGCSE Computer Studies.

Chapter 23 is written specifically for IGCSE Information Technology.

Computer Studies learning outcomes

In Chapters 16 to 22 of Section 6 you will learn the development stages of completing your coursework project. When you have finished Chapters 16 to 22 you will be able to:

* ❖ choose a suitable topic for your project;

* ❖ describe and evaluate the existing solution;

* ❖ consider alternative solutions;

* ❖ design, test and evaluate a new solution;

* ❖ provide the necessary technical and user documentation.

Information Technology learning outcomes

In Chapter 23 of Section 6 you will learn the development stages of completing your practical tests. When you have finished Chapter 23 you will be able to:

* ❖ assess your own progress in acquiring the skills needed for your practical tests;

* ❖ devise a revision strategy for the practical tests.

Differences between the Computer Studies project and the practical tests for Information Technology

There is a great deal of similarity and overlap between the specification for Computer Studies and that for Information Technology. The main differences involve systems analysis and the weighting given to practical/coursework elements. Systems analysis and the formulation of solutions to problems, including algorithms and programming languages, are studied in much more detail by Computer Studies students and are needed for the project work. The other major difference is concerned with assessment and the weighting given to the practical elements. For Computer Studies students the written examination accounts for 75% of the marks, whereas for Information Technology students the examination paper accounts for 40%. Therefore the Computer Studies project forms a less significant part of the overall assessment for each candidate than do the practical tests in Information Technology – 25% as opposed to 60%. In the Computer Studies coursework project the candidates are free to choose their own problem to solve and are free to use any suitable method of solution. This solution could be to write their own computer program in a programming language of their choice or they could use existing application software. In the Information Technology practical tests candidates have no choice of method of solution. They have to use whatever software is available in their school to carry out a series of tasks that are given in the form of examination papers. These tasks have to be completed in a fixed time period of 2¾ hours for each of two examination papers. The project for Computer Studies has no time limit and is an extended piece of work carried out over a period of time. The only time limit is an external moderation deadline, and the centre will need to set its own internal deadline in order to meet this moderation date.

16 Hardware and software

The definitions of hardware and software, together with specific examples of each, have been fully discussed in Sections 1–5. As preparation for the project you should make a detailed list of hardware and software available at your school. You will need to pay particular attention to peripheral devices and note the strengths and weaknesses of each particular device. This will enable you to select an appropriate input or output device for your problem. Similarly, noting the effectiveness of various applications software or any programming language will help you to select the most suitable software application as your method of solution.

In most solutions to problems, the keyboard will be the primary source of input data. However, you might wish to suggest using an alternative input method, such as a document reader, if you think that would improve your solution. You should also consider the minimum hardware specification, which is often determined by the particular operating system and software applications being used. This specification will include such items as the amount of random access memory (RAM), the speed of the processor and the capacity of the hard disk. The requirements of the system – whether it requires direct or serial access – will also determine the backing storage device and the corresponding medium to be used. Similarly, consideration needs to be given to the size and resolution of the display screen. The quality of any printed output you require will determine the type of printing device to be used. All of these hardware factors will be taken into consideration in determining the method of solution to your chosen problem.

There are similar things to consider when deciding what software to use. For example, you need to ask yourself 'Do I use an existing software application or do I write my own program?' If your answer is 'Write my own program', then the supplementary question might be 'Which language should I use?' This question will only be relevant if you have learnt more than one language. If your answer to the first question is 'Use an existing software application', then the supplementary question is 'Which software application should I use?'

One of the most interesting projects I have seen recently seen involved inventory/stock control and the associated invoicing system. You might assume that this problem would be solved by using a database application. However, the entire project was solved by using a spreadsheet in an imaginative way.

Task

1   Make a list of hardware configurations that are available.

2   Make a list of input devices that are available.

3   Make a list of printing devices that are available.

4   Make a list of any other hardware devices that are available and could be used.

5   For each item in the list, write down when each item would be used and any special requirements.

6   Copy your results into a table like Table 16.1.

Table 16.1 Characteristics of available hardware

Device	Type	Used for	Further information
Keyboard	Input	Entering data Controlling pointers by using ←,→,↑,↓ keys	
Plotter	Output	Producing charts, drawings, maps	Flatbed or drum

This table can be used later, once the objectives of the proposed solution have been set, to determine if the system hardware requirements can be met and a solution is possible.

7   Make a list of available applications software. Copy the information into a table like Table 16.2.

Table 16.2 Characteristics of available software

Software	Type	Used for	Further information Advantages/disadvantages
Visual Basic	Programming language	Can be used to create a specific database	
Microsoft FrontPage	Applications software	Designing web pages	

This table can be used later, once the objectives of the proposed solution have been set, to determine which software will be used to solve the problem.

17 Selecting the project

Perhaps the single most important piece of work that you will complete during the course is the coursework project for Computer Studies. You will also have to complete other practical activities which will prepare you for this task. One of the aims of the CIE Computer Studies syllabus is to 'develop students' abilities to solve problems using computing techniques'. Clearly the main form of assessment is by means of a single piece of coursework of a substantial nature. The assessment of your project involves three skills:

➢ knowledge and understanding;

➢ problem solving and realisation;

➢ communication.

You have a choice of both topic and software for your project in Computer Studies: you could choose to write your own computer program, so you will have to have some knowledge and experience of a computer programming language.

Your teacher can help you to overcome specific difficulties in various stages of the project in Computer Studies, provided such help is part of the normal teaching process and that once you have received it you are able to extend this work and build on the help that the teacher has given you.

Often the mark you are able to score in your coursework project is closely linked with your choice of problem to be solved. The Computer Studies project involves using a computer to solve a substantial problem, testing the solution on a computer system and thoroughly documenting the solution. Some topics and the associated method of solution make it difficult for you to score marks and satisfy some of the assessment criteria. In particular, a project that is a theoretical description of some aspect of problem solving produced using a word processor will score relatively low marks, unless the student writes and uses their own macros. In this latter case, the student would also have to fully document the structure and use of the macros. For previous examinations, some candidates have produced a thorough evaluation of a specific piece of applications software, comparisons of similar applications software or a user guide. While these projects may have been excellent examples of software evaluation or user guides, unfortunately there was never a real problem to solve, so many of the assessment criteria could not be met and the projects scored very few marks. It is essential that the project attempts to solve a particular problem and produces some actual output from the solution.

Many candidates are fortunate in having access to small businesses, and the better projects have a clearly defined purpose in the specific context of the chosen business.

You should note that your project is an individual project – group projects, or working on a joint project, are not allowed.

When choosing your problem to solve, you may wish to use the assessment criteria to determine if your problem will allow you to document each particular section. If your problem and/or chosen method of solution is unable to meet a significant number of assessment criteria, then perhaps you should reconsider your choice of problem. You should note that not every project will be capable of scoring marks in every section. For example, if you choose a problem for which there is no existing solution, then it automatically follows that you can not score marks for the description of the existing solution and the evaluation of the existing solution. Therefore, a total of four marks out of fifty are immediately unavailable. We hope you will use this information to ensure that the problem you choose for your project is suitable and offers an opportunity for further possible extension.

17.1 Suggestions for the Computer Studies project

You may choose to solve your problem either by using an existing software applications package or by writing your own program(s). The following list is offered as a suggestion but it is in no way complete and you are encouraged to think of your own problem:

➢ an inventory/stock control system;

➢ airline/theatre reservation system;

➢ cruise/holiday booking system;

➢ real estate agency;

➢ website design;

➢ computer-controlled greenhouse/lift/traffic lights/sensors;

➢ seat reservations systems;

> ➢ payroll/wages;

> ➢ doctor/dentist/hospital records;

> ➢ sports club/library club.

One of most important tasks is to complete the work in time, so it may be useful to devise a timetable, possibly using a Gantt chart/diagram. A Gantt chart is a graphical way of showing the time scale for your project. Table 17.1 is a simplified Gantt chart for the writing of this book.

Table 17.1
A Gantt chart

Activity	Month										
	1	2	3	4	5	6	7	8	9	10	11
Ideas	▓										
First draft		▓	▓	▓							
Proofreading					▓	▓					
Editing							▓	▓	▓		
Proofreading										▓	
Final editing											▓

If you incorporate a similar timetable into the documentation, it will earn credit in the appropriate section. Whatever topic you choose, you must include enough documentation on all aspects of the solution. Analysing the assessment criteria will reveal the importance of documentation. There are more marks for the analysis, testing and evaluation than the actual design phase.

Tasks

1   Make a list of topics that you think would form the basis for your project.

2   Identify a particular problem that you think might exist in these topics.

3   For each topic and associated problem, write down the way in which you will find the information you need to start your project.

4   Discuss these topics with your teacher and make a final decision on your choice of project.

18 Documenting the project

This chapter is only for the Computer Studies syllabus

An essential component of the solution to any problem is the documentation. You will have already studied systems analysis and the system life cycle in a theoretical context. It is now necessary to use that theory and put it into practice. The typical stages in the system life cycle are represented in Figure 18.1.

Figure 18.1
Stages in the system life cycle

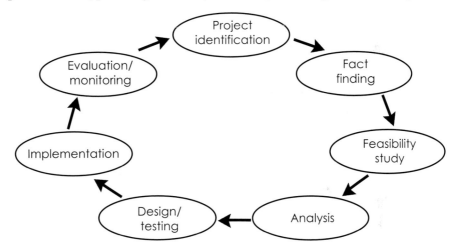

The stages are explained below:

➤ Project identification is where the problem is identified and defined. There may be existing evidence that a particular process is not working effectively – customers may have complained about a particular aspect or the management may have identified an area of the business that could be developed further.

➤ Fact finding is where investigations take place to collect information about the problem and how the current system deals with it.

➤ The feasibility study details the various costs and benefits of implementing a solution.

➤ The analysis stage is a full investigation of the complete system and will produce a specification.

> ➤ Design and testing is the actual process of producing a solution according to the specification derived from the analysis stage. Details of input requirements, processing, data structures, hardware and software requirements will be documented, together with back-up, security and data-recovery procedures.

> ➤ Implementation is the process by which the solution will be introduced into the business.

> ➤ Evaluation is the process that assesses the solution's effectiveness and examines what systems are in place to keep the solution working effectively if requirements change in the future.

In the world of business and commerce this work may be carried out within the company, if the company is sufficiently large to have a computer unit. In smaller companies this work will be contracted out to a specialist systems analyst. Each stage of this process needs to be thoroughly documented so that:

> ➤ the solution can be planned professionally;

> ➤ users can use the solution;

> ➤ we can maintain and develop the solution.

Such written documentation is vital because the systems analysts will produce a specification and many programmers will be involved in the modular design of the solution. Each programmer needs exact details of where their own particular module fits into the overall solution and has to work to specific input and output requirements so that the modules will all fit together to provide the overall solution.

In the context of your project, documentation is the only way you can show to the examination board that you have satisfied the requirement contained in the subject specification that you have used a computer to solve a specific problem and to document the solution. Marks can only be awarded for what is contained in the final documentation.

Documentation should include full details of each stage of the system life cycle together with technical documentation and user documentation.

18.1 Technical documentation

Technical documentation is written to provide a programmer or systems analyst with an explanation of how the system works. It should contain details of both the system hardware configuration and the software. Technical documentation comprises two main components:

> ➤ systems documentation, which describes the systems analysis, what is expected of the system, the overall design, the test plan and test data, together with the expected results;

> ➤ software documentation, which consists of a statement of the purpose of the software, any restrictions or limitations on the use of the software, the format for input data, the format for printed output, top-down design, program listings, data tables, data dictionaries, datafile specifications and any notes on any of these items that would assist in any future amendments.

18.2 User documentation

This is sometimes known as the user guide or user manual. This should include:

> ➤ an overview of what the solution does;

> ➤ details of how to install the solution;

> ➤ some examples of how certain functions work;

> ➤ information about what to do when certain errors occur;

> ➤ sample screen displays and/or output.

Documentation can be written in any style or format but it is recommended that you seriously consider structuring your documentation in a similar way to that of the assessment criteria. This will ensure that you have at least documented each section and should earn credit in each section.

18.3 Suggested framework for documenting the project

1   **Analysis**

1.1   Description of the problem

1.2   List of objectives

1.3   Description of existing solution

1.4   Evaluation of existing solution

1.5   Description of possible solutions

1.6   Evaluation of possible solutions

2   **Design**

2.1   Plan

2.2   Method of solution

2.3   Hardware requirements

2.4   Software requirements

3 Testing

3.1 Test strategy

3.2 Test results

4 Documentation

4.1 Technical documentation and system maintenance

4.2 User documentation

5 System evaluation and development

5.1 Evaluation

5.2 Future development/improvements

Notes: Each heading corresponding to a stage in the system life cycle, for example '1 Analysis', should start on a new page.

Use the automatic numbering facility of the word processor, as illustrated above, so that it is possible to refer to other sections of the documentation.

Make sure that your first page is a title page, followed by a contents page that lists all the headings and the relevant page numbers.

It is not our intention to produce an exemplar solution to a problem to illustrate what is required to document a project. This chapter has identified the important reasons for providing a fully documented solution to a problem. The following chapters will provide more details of what is required in each of the important areas of documentation.

Task

Using the suggested framework as a guide, design the framework and headings you will use to document your project.

19 Analysing the problem

This chapter is only for the Computer Studies syllabus

You will by now have chosen the topic or context for your project. It may be based on a real business or some aspect of school administration. It may involve helping a new business in some way, for example advertising or administration. At this stage you will also be in the final year of the course and you will have been set a deadline for the completion of the project.

Tasks

1 Chapter 18 suggested creating a timetable for your project. Complete a similar table for the main headings that you designed in Chapter 18 and then estimate how many weeks each section will take you to complete. Finally work out the completion dates for each stage. An example is given in Table 19.1.

Table 19.1 Example of a project completion timetable

Heading	Weeks	Completion date
Analysis	5	14 January
Design	3	5 February
Testing	1	12 February
Documentation	2	26 February
Evaluation	1	5 March

Note: The number of weeks and completion dates are not intended to represent time taken for a real project, they are simply used as examples.

2 Now compare the last completion date with the completion date set by your school. If your completion date is after the school's completion date, then you will have to alter your dates so that you are able to complete the project on time. It is advisable to make sure that your completion date is at least one week before the school's date. In this way you will allow yourself extra time just in case you need it on one or more of the sections.

3   You might wish to complete the table using all the headings and subheadings that you used in your framework design. Part of the table for the suggested framework has been completed for you (see Table 19.2).

Table 19.2   Part of a detailed timetable

Heading		Weeks	Completion date
1 Analysis			
	Description of the problem		
	List of objectives	1	17 December
	Description of existing solution		
	Evaluation of existing solution	2	31 December
	Description of possible solutions		
	Evaluation of possible solutions	2	14 January

Note: Remember that these timetables can be used as part of your plan for your project and should be included as part of the final documentation.

Every student will produce their own individual project and will need to develop their own documentation. However, there will be common features for the documentation of all projects. They also form the basis for the assessment of the project and the suggested framework for documentation. Many candidates fail to score marks for their project by leaving out sections of documentation or by not including enough details. Table 19.3 (overleaf) shows how marks are awarded in the analysis section of the scheme of assessment.

In order to maximise the marks that you score in your project, you should ask your teacher for a copy of the assessment grid. It is not our intention to produce a sample project for you. However it is our intention to let you know what should be included in the documentation of your project.

19.1 Description of the problem

Some candidates make little or no effort to describe the context for their project. Some candidates also fail to describe the nature of the problem they are attempting to solve. It is expected that the documentation will include a description of the organisation or business and the nature of the problem to be solved. You might wish to include details such as: business name; purpose of the business; what it does; where it is based; the number of workers the business employs.

Candidates are often confused between aims and objectives. The solution of the problem can be interpreted as the overall aim. The objectives are the details

Table 19.3 Analysis section of the scheme of assessment

Analysis	1 mark	2 marks	3 marks
1 Description of the problem	Brief description of the background to the business or organisation	Description of the background to the business or organisation, together with the nature of the problem to be solved	
2 Objectives (must be stated in relation to the proposed solution)	Objectives listed in general business terms, e.g. to make a process faster, to save time or resources	Objectives listed in computer-related terms, e.g. create a database, sort, search a database, edit a record, etc.	Objectives listed in both general business terms and computer-related terms
3 Description of existing solution	Incomplete description of the current solution	A full description of the current solution, including data input requirements (data-capture methods and data dictionary, if applicable) and specifications, the data processing and output requirements and specifications	
4 Evaluation of existing solution	Incomplete evaluation	Complete evaluation highlighting advantages, disadvantages and suggested improvements	
5 Description of other possible solutions, (including the proposed solution)	Description of one other possible solution, i.e. the proposed solution	Description of at least two other possible solutions, including the proposed new solution	
6 Evaluation of other possible solutions	Evaluation of the advantages and disadvantages of the alternative solutions	Evaluation of the advantages and disadvantages of the alternative solutions. The choice of proposed solution should be justified	

of how these general aims will be achieved. For example, an aim might be to create a membership list that can be used to aid the administration of an organisation. There are many ways that this could be achieved, but the objectives might include the use of a database management system to create a data table and the mail-merge facility of a word processor applications software.

19.2 List of objectives

Without knowing the nature of the problem to be solved and the detailed objectives to be achieved, it is very difficult, if not impossible, to evaluate the success or failure of the candidate's solution. One particular area of weakness in the documentation of projects is candidates' failure to specify clear objectives. Often candidates specify their objective as being to make a particular process faster, to save time or to save resources. No mention is made of how this will be achieved. Taking the objective 'to make a particular process faster' as an example, in order to evaluate the project we would need to know, and compare, how long the process takes before the candidate's solution and how long the process takes after the candidate's solution. Such timings will have to be part of the testing strategy and it is very rare that such testing is ever documented. Objectives should be interpreted as relating to data-processing requirements or computer-related activities; for example, to create a data table, to create a website, to edit a record, to insert email facility on a web form, etc. Each one of these objectives can easily be tested by producing some hard copy output. Particular emphasis must be made on specifying the objectives because subsequent parts of the scheme of assessment refer back to these objectives. Not only will you lose the marks in this section if you do not state your objectives in the specified manner, but you will also lose marks in the planning, testing and evaluation sections.

19.3 Description of existing solution

You should remember that some problems may not have an existing solution, so it will not be possible to score marks in this section or for evaluating the current solution. If a current solution exists, then it will be possible to describe the flow of data within the solution. This can be described in either words or diagrams, both of which should demonstrate the concept of an I–P–O (input–process–output) model. The main requirements that need to be documented are the detailed input specifications, data-capture methods, data-processing techniques, storage requirements and the output specifications. Examples of data-capture forms and hard copy output should also be included.

19.4 Evaluation of existing solution

The advantages and disadvantages, the strengths and weaknesses of the existing solution should be discussed. These should be specifically linked to the overall problem to be solved. There may well be some other strengths or weaknesses that are not related to this particular problem, but for the purpose of the project these are not important and should not be discussed.

19.5 Description of possible solutions

There will usually be more than one way to solve a problem and the Computer Studies project is no exception. Many candidates consider three possible solutions:

➢ extending any current, often paper-based, system;

➢ using a software application package;

➢ either using a second software application package or using a programming language to write a custom solution.

Candidates must discuss their proposed solution and preferably at least one other solution. Using a second possible solution will allow some evaluation to take place.

19.6 Evaluation of possible solutions

The advantages and disadvantages, the strengths and weaknesses of the various possible solutions should be discussed. These should be specifically linked to the overall problem to be solved. Candidates are expected to justify their choice of proposed solution. A particular solution can be justified by giving the reasons for its selection. This can easily be achieved by the use of a sentence that begins 'I have chosen to use … because …'.

Task

Using your framework, which you developed at the end of Chapter 18, insert subheadings to indicate what should be included in each section. You may wish to consider using a different coloured font for these notes; this will remind you that these notes can be deleted once you have completed each section.

20 Designing and implementing the solution

Now that the analysis of the problem has been completed and objectives set, it is possible to develop the solution, look at other possible solutions and plan a schedule for the completion of your project.

The importance of setting objectives has already been discussed as being the basis of your project. These objectives are needed now in order to plan your work. You will have already completed a preliminary timetable, but you will now have to finalise the plan. Table 20.1 shows how marks are awarded in the design section of the scheme of assessment.

Table 20.1 Design section of the scheme of assessment

Design	1 mark	2 marks	3 marks	4 marks
7 Plan	Incomplete or unclear plan	Detailed plan, including time schedule	Detailed plan, time schedule clearly linked to objectives in section 2	
8 Description of the method of solution. This could be in the form of top-down design, structure diagrams, flowcharts or pseudocode	Unclear or confused method of solution	Clear method of solution but some aspects of the method of solution are missing	Clear and detailed description of the method of solution, including database tables, any relationships	
9 Hardware	Incomplete list of hardware	A complete list of hardware	A detailed specification	A detailed specification together with at least two reasons why such hardware is needed in the context of the proposed solution
10 Software	List of software used	Description of the software used	Justification of why this software is being used or written	

Once you have decided what problem you are going to solve and how this solution will be achieved (the objectives), you need to plan the order in which the activities will be carried out and to assess how long it will take. Candidates often fail to include in their documentation any indication of their plan of action. If the objectives have been listed in a logical order, then the plan will automatically follow the sequence of your objectives. If they haven't, then the objectives need to be sorted into a logical order of completing the tasks and this will be the plan. You will now realise the importance of numbering your objectives so that you can make frequent reference to them in this section and in later sections.

The analysis section will have determined your overall method of solution. However, this now needs to be broken down into much more detail. It is from this information that a solution will be constructed. You will need to show the overall design, possibly by using a system diagram or top-down design which will describe the solution. You may decide to use alternative methods of describing this solution using flowcharts or pseudocode. It must show how you may have broken down the problem into smaller modules, and how these modules fit together. You will need to specify the input and output requirements and specifications. Data structures used and data storage should also be discussed. Up until this point, the documentation should be capable of being used to solve the problem by either writing your own program or by using an applications package.

You will be using a computer to solve your problem and you will need to specify the hardware needed for your solution. The minimum hardware needed may be a lower specification than the computer that you actually used. If it is, you will need to investigate the minimum specification needed for your operating system and any software used and to make allowances for the memory requirements of your data in terms of random access memory and backing store capacity. The higher marks can only be achieved if the documentation includes a full technical specification and some justification as to why such hardware is needed. Usually such justification involves the use of peripherals over and above what might be considered a standard specification for a personal computer, or the need for a large random access memory or large backing storage capacity.

Finally, the choice of software needs to be discussed and reasons given as to why that particular software has been used. It is not a sufficient reason to say 'it's the only software we have'. It is often useful to mention the specific features of the software that enable the objectives to be achieved. Table 20.2 shows how marks are awarded in the implementation section of the scheme of assessment.

Table 20.2 Implementation section of the scheme of assessment

Implementation	1 mark	2 marks
11 Method of solution related to the problem by suitable means, including the use of annotated listings or pseudocode	Method of solution described in generic terms	Method of solution described in specific details relevant to the problem
12 Accurate method of solution	Partly successful, some objectives achieved as listed previously	Completely successful, all objectives achieved as listed previously

Although this section of the scheme of assessment has been reproduced, you don't need to provide any further documentation. The purpose of this section is to allow your teachers to assess your method of solution in an additional way. It is important to note that all documentation should be specific to your problem and your solution. Most teachers provide notes for guidance for you to document your project – this is a normal part of the teaching process. However, if your teacher does provide this guidance, then you must rewrite any notes in your own words and make it specific to your problem. In the past it has been noted that, in some sections, the majority of work from some centres was virtually identical and candidates had made no attempt to rewrite these sections in their own words. In these circumstances, the marks for these sections will be reduced to zero for all candidates concerned.

21 | Testing and evaluating the project

> This chapter is only for the Computer Studies syllabus

You are now in, what you hope, are the final stages of your project. Whether you are or not will depend on the success of what you have achieved so far. Your testing might discover that some sections need to be improved. It is very rare, though not impossible, for a solution to work first time. Table 21.1 shows how marks are awarded in the testing section of the scheme of assessment.

Table 21.1   Testing section of the scheme of assessment

Testing	1 mark	2 marks	3 marks	4 marks
13 Test strategy	Incomplete test strategy, which should include the data to be tested together with the expected results	Complete test strategy, which should include the data to be tested together with the expected results	Complete test strategy, which should include the data to be tested together with the expected results and linked to the objectives in section 2	
14 Test results (normal, extreme and abnormal data)	One type of data tested	Two types of data tested	All three types of data tested	All three types of data tested and linked to the objectives in section 2

Many candidates produce pages and pages of testing but provide no indication of what is being tested. Given the scope of the project, it is not expected that every single possibility is to be tested. What is important is that every type of data has been tested in several situations, in terms of input and processing.

It is important that the test strategy is documented before the actual test results are obtained. This is another section where it is important to refer back to the original objectives. You may find it useful to use a table format, including columns for objective number, purpose, test data and expected result, to specify their test strategy.

However, a table format is not recommended for the actual test results since it is not clear whether or not such results have actually been obtained by using the solution. It might be assumed by a moderator that a results table has been word processed. It is important to remember that a computer must be used to solve a problem and it should be clear from the documentation that more than just a word processor has been used. One of the best ways of proving that the solution has been implemented is to include a number of screen dumps that show data actually being input. Many candidates claim to have tested for abnormal data but often provide no real proof in their documentation. Providing screen dumps is essential in this case since one screen dump can be used to provide evidence of the data input and a second can be used to provide evidence of the error message produced by its rejection.

Candidates are often not sure what evidence to provide in their testing section. If one objective was to create a database, then it is expected that there will be some evidence that a database had been created. There should be examples of: data-capture forms – blank forms and completed forms; any data-capture screen; printed evidence of a data table. If another objective was to edit records, then the record should be printed before editing, the changes to be made should be specified and the record printed after the change, highlighting where the change has occurred. If one objective was to create a web page, then the design should be drawn together with a printed screen dump of the actual page. If an objective was to provide links to other pages either in the same site or in an external site, then screen dumps should be printed to show these links. In these circumstances, where it is difficult for candidates to produce printed evidence of the actual link being achieved, it will be necessary for the teacher to certify that the link has been successful.

You should understand that there are three general categories of test data:

➢ Normal data – This is valid data in a range that the program is designed to handle.

➢ Extreme data – This is still valid data. It is normal data at the limits of acceptability.

➢ Abnormal data – This is invalid data. The programmer must assume that sooner or later users will attempt to enter invalid data, and the program must not as a consequence 'crash' or give wrong results. Therefore such data should be rejected.

Unfortunately, many candidates show their lack of understanding of extreme and abnormal data. In the context of numbers within the range 0 to 100 inclusive: the extreme data would be both 0 and 100, the maximum and minimum values; normal data would be any number between 1 and 99; abnormal data would be any number outside this range, any negative number or number greater than 100, or any alphabetic or other symbol/character.

In the context of a single alphabetic value: the extreme data would be both a and z; the normal data would be any letter between b and y; abnormal data would be any number or any other character.

Once the actual test results have been achieved, then the evaluation of the project is a very simple task. Again, this is another section where it is important to refer back to the original objectives. It is also important in this section to refer back to the test strategy and the test results. Using the objectives numbers as a guideline, it should now be a simple task to compare the actual results from the test results section with the expected results from the test strategy section. If the test results are the same as the expected results, then that objective has been achieved. It is important to realise that the project does not have to be entirely successful to earn full marks in the evaluation section.

All solutions will be capable of further extension or further development. You may wish to add a new feature to the current capabilities, or an improved method of data input, or alternative peripheral devices might offer some possibilities. You do not have to implement these improvements, you only have to make some reasonable sensible suggestions. Table 21.2 shows how marks are awarded in the evaluation section of the scheme of assessment.

Table 21.2   Evaluation section of the scheme of assessment

System evaluation and development	1 mark	2 marks	3 marks
17 Evaluation	Inaccurate or trivial evaluation	Reasonable evaluation	Reasonable evaluation linked to the objectives in section 2
18 Developments (the candidate does not necessarily have to be capable of carrying out these suggestions)	Some improvements suggested	Realistic and meaningful suggestions for development	

22 Technical and user documentation

The final part of the solution is concerned with both user and technical documentation. The user documentation or user guide contains the important details that the user would need in order to operate the system. The technical documentation contains information that would be needed to maintain the system. Table 22.1 shows how marks are awarded in the documentation section of the scheme of assessment.

Table 22.1 Documentation section of the scheme of assessment

	1 mark	2 marks	3 marks
15 Technical documentation	Inadequate documentation	Satisfactory documentation which would enable maintenance or modification of the system.	
16 User documentation	Inadequate or unclear details	Clear details but incomplete	Clear and complete user guide

22.1 Technical documentation

The technical documentation section is required so that the system could be maintained or changed in some way. Some of this information may have already been documented in earlier sections, but it is often better to repeat the details in this specific section. Technical documentation should include:

➢ title

➢ purpose

➢ author

➢ hardware and software used

➢ file and table specifications

➢ restrictions or limitations

➢ formulas/equations used

> ➢ procedures specified

> ➢ structure charts/flowcharts/top-down design

> ➢ annotated listings.

22.2 User documentation

The user guide should provide information that shows a potential user how to use the system. This includes:

> ➢ the hardware and software requirements;

> ➢ how to install the solution;

> ➢ how to enter, edit and save data;

> ➢ how to process and output data;

> ➢ how problems might be avoided;

> ➢ how to cope with any problems that may arise.

It is also useful to include examples of screen displays that show how to do some of these things. Your user guide should cover all aspects of the solution from data input to data output. Sample runs showing the whole process provide an ideal opportunity to demonstrate how to operate the system. One way to make sure that your user guide is of a high standard is to ask another student to use the instructions to operate the system. Often the user is asked to comment on the quality of the user documentation – these comments could be included as part of the user guide. For example, the user could comment on the usefulness of your instructions to perform a certain task or the clarity of your back-up procedures.

We have now covered all aspects of the project and its documentation. Remember that marks can only be awarded if there is hard copy proof of what you have done. It is advisable that you make back-up copies of your work but do not submit a floppy disk or CD. Only the printed work will be marked by your teacher and by the moderator. Good luck with your project. If you use the advice in this chapter, you will document your project in a systematic way and will score marks at every opportunity.

23 Practical assessments for Information Technology

This chapter is only for the Information Technology syllabus

Practical skills are an important part of the assessment for IGCSE Information Technology. These skills count for 60% of the examination, so it is vital that you are fully prepared for the test and have mastered all the required skills.

The skills are divided into eight objective areas, A1–A8, with each area being split into smaller sub-objectives. Each specific objective has clear guidance on what you are expected to achieve in terms of the performance criteria and the skills that you have to demonstrate in order to satisfy the performance criteria. Each assessment objective is related to a particular software application and these are specified in the assessment criteria for practical tests. As a specific example, Table 23.1 shows part of the assessment objective A2 needed in document production.

Table 23.1   Assessment objective A2: document production

Students should be able to use word processing facilities to prepare documents.
Using word processing facilities, the candidate must demonstrate the ability to:

Specific objectives	Performance criteria	Skills
3 Enter data from different sources		
3.1 Load data from existing files	3.1.1 Specified file is loaded	
3.2 Key in text and numbers	3.2.1 Text and numbers are entered as specified with no more than 3 errors	Enter text, enter numbers
3.3 Import image from external source	3.3.1 Place image as specified	Import clip art, import from a digital source, import from file, import from website
	3.3.2 Manipulate as specified	Move image, resize image, crop image, text wrap
3.4 Include information downloaded from the Internet	3.4.1 Specified data only, positioned as required	Text, graphic image, table, chart
4 Document format		
4.1 Set up a page format	4.1.1 Page size as specified	
	4.1.2 Page orientation as specified	Portrait, landscape
	4.1.3 Page numbering as specified and positioned consistently	Header, footer
	4.1.4 Margins set as specified	Top margin, bottom margin, left margin, right margin
	4.1.5 Line spacing as specified	Single, 1.5 times, double
	4.1.6 Alignment set as specified	Left, centered, right, fully justified
5 Text appearance and layout		
5.1 Use indentation	5.1.1 Specified portion of text only hanging indent	Indent text, indent paragraph,
5.2 Use bullet points	5.2.1 Specified portion of text only	Bulleted list
5.3 Use tables	5.3.1 Table inserted as specified	Specified number of rows and columns
5.4 Control pages	5.4.1 Breaks inserted as specified	Page break, widows, orphans
5.5 Use fonts	5.5.1 Font size as specified	Point size, increase, decrease

We shall use this particular assessment objective to demonstrate how you could prepare for the examination. The skills you need can be organised into another table, which you can then use to record your progress (see Table 23.2).

Table 23.2 Recording your progress

Objective	Skills	Tick when complete	Exam preparation
3.1 Load data from existing file	Load a specific file		
3.2 Key in data	Enter text and numbers		
3.3 Import image	Import clip art Import digital picture Import picture file Import picture from website		
3.3 Manipulate image	Move image Resize image Crop image Use text wrap		
3.4 Download from the Internet	Text Graphic image Table Chart		

When you have mastered each individual skill, you can place a tick in column 3. The last column is for examination preparation. Having mastered all the individual and specific skills, you need to combine them and apply them in an integrated way. The best way to practise this is to do an integrated task that tests your skills in the same way that the actual practical tests will. Ask your teacher for an integrated task or use the task that follows. When you have done an integrated task and can master a particular skill, then you can put a tick the appropriate box in column 4.

23.1 Practice assessments

It is good practice for you to experience as many practical assessments under examination conditions as possible.

Task

Use the assessment criteria in the IGCSE Information Technology syllabus and your document production skills, assessment objective A2, to produce a grid similar to Table 23.1. This will allow you to assess your progress as you acquire the specific skills. You may wish to work together with other students and share this task. You could then use your communication skills, assessment objective A1, to send the grids as attachments in an email to the rest of the group.

Sample practical assessment

The following is intended to simulate one of your practical assessments. It is not possible to simulate every possible aspect but at least it will give you an indication of some the tasks you are expected to complete.

Communication

1   Send an email to one of your fellow students. Ask them to use the Google search engine and keyword ICT. Select the image tab and ask them to send you the URL address of the ICT for Learning Project graphic. If for any reason this graphic is no longer available when you practise this exercise, ask them to use any suitable graphic.

2   When you receive a reply from your friend, download the graphic and send it to your friend as an attachment.

3   Print the contents of your email (before you send it) so that it clearly shows that the attachment is present.

Document production

4   Ask your teacher to provide an unformatted text file. If this is not possible, then type in some of your notes from one of your GCSE subjects.

5   Format the document to A4 size and portrait.

6   Insert your name at the bottom of each page and the page number at the top of each page.

7   Set the page margins – top, bottom, left and right – to 2.5 centimetres.

8   Set the text to double line spacing, right aligned and 14 point.

9   Insert a suitable heading at the top of the document. Centre the heading and change the font size and type and increase to 16 point.

10   Insert suitable subheadings.

11   Add some bullet points that summarise the contents to the bottom of the document and indent by 1 centimetre.

12   After your bullet points, insert a table that repeats the bullet points.

13   Make sure your document has no spelling mistakes and save it.

14   Print a draft copy of the document.

Data manipulation

15 Ask your teacher for a datafile.

16 Insert three extra records.

17 Edit two records.

18 Save the data and print a draft copy.

19 Design a report which satisfies the following criteria:

- all data is shown;

- sorted in ascending order of one of the fields;

- page orientation is set to landscape;

- includes a title and today's date.

20 Save and print the report.

21 Design a new report that satisfies a criterion of your choice, and which also satisfies the following criteria:

- shows only selected fields (must include the field for your chosen criterion);

- sorted into descending order;

- includes a calculated total.

22 Save and print this report.

23 Repeat 21, but save the data in a form that can be imported into your text document.

Integration

24 Open your text document from 13.

25 Insert your graphic from 2 and make sure it is in the top left-hand corner of the document.

26 Insert your data from 23 and make sure it is at the end of the document.

27 Insert a page break immediately before the table from 12.

Data modelling/analysis

28   Create a data model based on the following:

Import duty						
Country of origin	Cost	Quantity	Total cost	Import tax	Post and packing	TOTAL

Notes: *Shaded cell will contain the percentage import duty to be paid if the country of origin is not UK.*

Cost column will contain the cost for each item.

Quantity will indicate how many items have been purchased.

29   In the cell under 'Total cost' insert a formula that calculates cost multiplied by quantity.

30   In the cell under 'Import tax' insert a formula that contains zero if Country of origin is UK and calculates Total cost multiplied by percentage import duty if the Country of origin is not UK.

31   In the cell under 'Post and packing' insert a formula that calculates Total cost × by 0.08 if the Country of origin is UK and calculates 10 + (Total cost × 0.08) if the Country of origin is not UK.

32   In the cell under TOTAL insert a formula that adds together the Total cost, Import tax and Post and packing.

33   Format the Import duty as a percentage with three decimal places.

34   Format any cells that contain a cost as dollars.

35   Format the Quantity cells as integer.

36   Replicate all formulas to give 15 rows of data.

37   Choose a suitable page orientation so as to select a view that shows all formulas.

38   Enter data with an import duty of 7.5% and 12 items with a country of origin, cost and quantity of your choice. Make sure that you include UK at least four times, China twice and Pakistan once.

39   Save this data and print a copy, making sure that it will fit on one page.

40   Print a copy selecting only those rows where the Country of origin is UK.

41   Print a copy selecting those rows that are either China or Pakistan.

Web design

42 Using a suitable package, create styles that you can use throughout this website. Save the style sheet and attach to each web page.

H1 Arial bold centre

H2 Arial bold

H3 Arial italic

P Times New Roman

L same as H3.

43 Create a new home page that has a heading at the top, menu options on the right and a text/graphics area on the left. It should look like this.

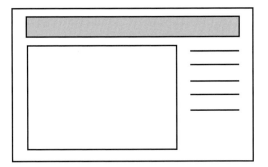

44 Type in the name of your school into the heading, using style H1.

45 Type in a menu consisting of a heading (style H2) and links to two other pages.

46 Create the links to these other two pages.

47 Open one of these two pages.

48 Insert a table with two rows and three columns.

49 Merge columns 1 and 2, insert a graphic.

50 Insert a title in column 3 row 1, style P.

51 Insert your name in the remaining cell, style L.

52 Insert a link to return to your home page.

53 Open the other blank page.

54 Insert three rows of text and a link to your home page.

55 Save all your work.

56 Print all the pages.

7 Revision and examination questions

> ## Learning outcomes
>
> Section 7 is devoted entirely to revision and examination questions. These will help you gain experience in answering examination questions. All questions are suitable for either Computer Studies or Information Technology, except where indicated otherwise.
>
> When you have finished this section you will be able to:
>
> ❖ devise a revision strategy;
>
> ❖ answer examination questions;
>
> ❖ identify any topic areas where you need further revision.

Revision

Everybody will need to revise before they sit the examination. It is essential that you plan your revision carefully and have a well-organised set of notes. You will have notes from school and you will probably make additional notes while using this textbook. First you will need to organise these notes into topics.

You will need to devise a timetable for your revision, outlining which topic you will revise when. As the examination gets nearer, you will need to test yourself regularly. You will find a selection of examination papers in this section. There are also additional questions that have been grouped into topics. When you want to revise a particular topic, you can use the questions in the relevant chapter or the topic questions from this section. When you want to revise the whole syllabus, use the examination papers from this section.

We have added suggested answers for two of the papers (Papers A and D). We recognise that English is not the first language of the vast majority of students, so we have given some alternative answers that are often just a different way of saying the same thing. We have written our suggested answers in brief note form so that we can provide this variety of possible answers. Where there is more than one answer on a line separated by a ' / ', then only one of these possible answers should be given in an examination.

Examination technique

First, read through all the questions before trying to answer any of them. After you have read all the questions, you should then begin to answer them, starting with the one that you find easiest. Read each question very carefully before you try to answer it. If you cannot answer a question, then move on to the next one. You should have time to go back and answer any previously unanswered questions. It is preferable for your answers to be in the form of short sentences, when appropriate. However, you could answer the questions in note form and this would be acceptable – the most import thing is to include the correct technical terms and/or key words or phrases.

It is important that you actually answer the question. Sometimes candidates try to answer by using similar words to the question. For example, if the question asks 'What is a relational database?', it is not acceptable to answer 'A database with relationships'.

You should also look carefully at how many marks are allocated to each part of the question. Usually you need to make one distinct or different point for each available mark. If the question asks for two reasons, then you must give two different answers. If you can, you might want to give three reasons, just in case two of your reasons are not considered to be different. (In the examination questions in this book we haven't given the marks available for each question; this is to encourage you to write down as many possible answers as you can.)

Which syllabus?

CS

Some questions are only relevant for the Computer Studies syllabuses. These are marked by this symbol in the margin.

24 Examination papers

24.1 Paper A

| CS | 1   Explain, using examples if appropriate, the meaning of these computer terms:

(a) random access memory (RAM)
(b) fax
(c) validation
(d) user documentation
(e) interrupt
(f) virtual reality

Suggested answers

(a) RAM:
- memory that can be read from / written to
- temporary memory / storage while power is on
- volatile memory / contents lost when power turned off

(b) Fax:
- document / message / picture sent by telephone line
- scanned image transmitted over ordinary telephone line
- photocopy transmitted by telephone

(c) Validation:
- check on data input
- detect data that is unreasonable
- ensure that data is reasonable / of the correct type
- uses range checks, check digits, batch totals, control totals, checksum

(d) User documentation:
- information needed to run software successfully
- how to run / load / save the program
- installing extra hardware needed
- installing extra software / extra copies
- identifying / correcting errors
- sample runs / input and output screens
- online help / tutorials

(e) Interrupt:
  - a signal generated by a device, causing a break in the execution of a program
  - allows peripherals to run independently, only sending data when they need to communicate with the central processor
  - use of stack
  - allows other routines to run

(f) Virtual reality:
  - use of software plus headgear / gloves to create / recreate an environment
  - computer controlled graphics to simulate the real world / 3D world

Note: Games would not be an acceptable answer.

CS

2 State **three** tasks that an operating system does for the user.

Suggested answers
  - handles user accounts
  - communicates directly with the user
  - load – save – run – rename – copy files
  - run / list programs / runs antivirus software
  - displays error messages / deals with errors
  - controls peripherals
  - organises files
  - start up / booting the system
  - control security
  - interrupt handling
  - organises use of main store between OS and the user

3 (a) Hackers gain illegal access to computer systems and may change and copy data.
State **two** effects of computer hacking.

(b) State two ways that users can protect their computer systems from hacking.

Suggested answers
(a)
  - virus introduced into the system
  - fraud / extortion / industrial espionage / bribery
  - processing time lost / system closes down
  - commercial sabotage (e.g. website crashes)
  - loss of business confidence

(b)
  - passwords for users and/or files
  - PIN / passwords changed frequently
  - encryption of files
  - disconnection after three unsuccessful attempts
  - set user access rights
  - firewalls

4   (a)   Describe **one** precaution that should be taken against loss of data in a batch processing system.

(b)   State two reasons why batch processing is more appropriate than real-time processing for dealing with electricity bills.

Suggested answers

(a)   ◆   back-ups / file generations
      ◆   parallel system

(b)   ◆   no immediate need for the results / not used as input for another process
      ◆   sensible to process all the data at the same time
      ◆   large amounts of data to be processed on a regular basis
      ◆   processing only needed at the end of month / week
      ◆   large number of bills
      ◆   no need for anyone to be present when the job is processed
      ◆   no need for user to communicate when the job is being run
      ◆   batch processing can be done overnight

5   The following spreadsheet shows the destination of people who travelled in Speedwell Taxis during a week.

	A	B	C	D	E	F
1		School	Shops	Station	Other	Total
2	Monday	6	4	2	4	16
3	Tuesday	4	3	3	4	14
4	Wednesday	6	5	3	6	20
5	Thursday	5	6	1	4	16
6	Friday	3	7	4	6	20
7	Saturday	4	6	6	8	24
8	Sunday	0	2	3	7	12
9	Total	28	33	22	39	122
10	Percentage	23	27	18	32	100
11						

(a)   Circle and clearly label on the diagram a **cell** which should contain a
      (i) label,
      (ii) value,
      (iii) formula.

(b)   Shade on the spreadsheet the **cells** which would be needed to produce a labelled pie chart showing the number of people travelling to the station that week.

(c)   Describe **two** more columns that could be added to the spreadsheet to enable extra calculations to be done.

Suggested answers

(a) (i) label – any cell in range A2:A10 or range B1:F1

(ii) value – any cell in range B2:E8

(iii) formula – any cell in range B9:F9 or range B10:F10 or range F2:F10

Note: Circle only one cell for each type – more than one cell selected would score 0.

(b) cells D2:D8

(c) ♦ distance travelled

♦ amount of money taken

♦ number of taxis available

♦ one of: average cost per journey on a particular day

cost per mile

average cost per journey to a particular place

Note: Average is not an acceptable answer but it may be allowed if you refer to a possible valid column.

6 A school office sells stationery items to pupils. A database is used to keep details of the stock. Part of the database is shown below.

CODE	ITEM	INSTOCK	SOLD	ONORDER	PRICE($)
C 302	Floppy disk	24	16	20	1.50
G 101	Rubber	16	14	10	1.00
G 102	Pen	18	22	20	2.00
G 103	Pencil	5	25	30	1.00
M 101	Protractor	8	12	20	1.50
M 202	Compass	8	12	20	2.00

(a) Suggest **two** more fields that could be used in this database.

(b) List the **ITEM**s output if the following search condition is used.

(**CODE** contains "**M**") or (**INSTOCK** < 15)

(c) Describe how you would sort the records into alphabetical order of **ITEM** field.

Suggested answers

(a) ♦ cost price / selling price

♦ supplier code / supplier contact details

♦ re-order level

♦ date of next order / order date

♦ price of each item / unit of stock

♦ tax – total cost / total price

♦ order number

(b) pencil, protractor, compass

(c) ♦ select sort from the menu

♦ select the ITEM field

♦ choose ascending order

7   A hospital uses a computer system to store details about the patients.
  (a) List **three** fields that would be in a patient's record, in addition to their name and address.
  (b) The doctors read the patient medical histories on their computer screens before treating the patients.
       (i) Describe **two** checks that should be done by a doctor to make sure that they have the correct patient record on the screen.
       (ii) State the type of file access that would be used by this system and give a reason why.
  (c) Patient records need to be amended, deleted and inserted. Give an example of why each of these would be needed.
  (d) Describe **three** data protection laws that may apply to patient data.
  (e) Describe **two** additional tasks that the hospital computer could do.

Suggested answers

(a) ♦ patient ID
    ♦ doctor ID
    ♦ gender
    ♦ DoB
    ♦ contact details/next of kin
    ♦ blood group
    ♦ date of last visit
    ♦ admission date
    ♦ previous illness
    ♦ photograph
    ♦ insurance company
    ♦ symptoms
    ♦ religion

Note: Age, heart / breathing rate, name, address would not *be acceptable answers.*

(b) (i) ♦ ask patient's name
       ♦ check symptoms match
       ♦ check DoB match
       ♦ check identity tag
       ♦ check photograph
    (ii) ♦ random access / direct access
       ♦ indexed sequential access
       ♦ reason: record needs to retrieved immediately
                  immediate updating

(c) *amended*
       ♦ change of name / address
       ♦ spelling mistake / data input error

deleted

- ◆ no longer needs treatment
- ◆ moved away
- ◆ died

inserted

- ◆ new patient moved into area
- ◆ first admission
- ◆ newborn baby

(d) ◆ data must be up to date
- ◆ data can only be used for that purpose
- ◆ data must be accurate
- ◆ data must be destroyed when no longer needed
- ◆ data user must be registered
- ◆ only authorised persons allowed access to data / data should not be disclosed to unauthorised persons
- ◆ data must be used fairly and lawfully

(e) ◆ monitoring patient condition / blood sampling
- ◆ controlling administration / stock control of drugs
- ◆ body scanner
- ◆ radiation doses
- ◆ meals service
- ◆ accounts
- ◆ salaries
- ◆ expert diagnostic system
- ◆ email / appointments systems / reminders / duty lists
- ◆ control equipment such as: air conditioning / environmental controls / alarm systems / burglar alarms

8 Students now use computer-based information retrieval systems to view data for topics they are studying rather than using textbooks.

(a) State **two** advantages to students of being able to do this.

(b) Describe **two** ways of reducing the cost of obtaining such computerised information.

Suggested answers

(a) ◆ wider range / large amount of information is available
- ◆ interactive method of learning
- ◆ specialists in each field can be consulted / specialist sites
- ◆ learn using multimedia
- ◆ up-to-date information
- ◆ access to databases worldwide
- ◆ faster search facilities

(b) ◆ restrict access to certain times of day
- ◆ evening / weekend phone calls are usually cheaper

- restrict site access
- download and then retrieve data offline
- use text-only format / no graphics, pictures, sounds or video
- faster modem / broadband
- compress files before downloading

9 A craftsman is using computer-aided design (CAD) software to produce a new design for a teapot.

(a) State **three** suitable input devices other than a keyboard and a mouse.

(b) State **three** features of the CAD software that makes it suitable for designing teapots.

Suggested answers

(a) • graphics tablet / digitiser
- light pen
- digital camera
- scanner

Note: Touch screen, or voice would not *be acceptable answers.*

(b) • accurate scale drawings / 3D drawings
- easy modification of images on screen
- can use image bank / library of shapes
- images saved to disk
- apply shades / colours
- draws polygons, curves, arcs, circles, etc.
- scale objects / zoom facility
- rotate objects / view from any angle
- can use real-world co-ordinates / actual measurements
- link to CAM

CS | **10** Read this algorithm.

```
Value = 0
Next-value = 0
input Value
input Next-value
while Next-value is not equal to zero do
    if Next-value is greater than Value then
        Value is equal to Next-value
    endif
    input Next-value
endwhile
output Value
```

(a) What is the output if the following numbers are input?
5, 4, 8, 3, 0, 23

(b) Write a modified algorithm to solve the same problem but always end after four numbers have been input.

Suggested answers

(a) 8

(b)

```
        Value = 0
        Next-value = 0
        input Value
        input Next-value
*       Counter = 2
*       while Counter is not greater than 4 do
            if Next-value is greater than Value then
            Value is equal to Next-value
            endif
*           add 1 to Counter
            input Next-value
*       endwhile
        output Value
```

Note: Changes are only necessary to lines marked *. Marks are likely to be awarded for initialising variables, setting up a loop, incrementing the counter.

11 A supermarket has decided to change from a manual order processing system to a computerised one.
(a) Describe **three** methods of fact finding that should be used.
(b) The new computerised system has been installed. Describe **two** ways in which the training of staff to use the new system might be done.

Suggested answers

(a) ◆   observations
     ◆   interview management / workers
     ◆   questionnaires / surveys
     ◆   look at order records
(b) ◆   learn software from a course or from an experienced user
     ◆   trial run using software prior to full installation
     ◆   use of CD-ROM / multimedia training package / CAL

Note: User guide, how to use onscreen help, expert system would not be acceptable answers.

CS

12 A credit card company keeps its customer account details in a master file. When a customer wants to purchase an item in a shop the customer card is swiped through a card reader. The company's computer first checks to see if the card is stolen. If it is not stolen the computer then checks to see if the amount of the purchase is less than or equal to the amount of money that the customer is allowed to spend. If so an authorisation code is sent to the shop and the purchase is completed, otherwise the request is cancelled.

Design an algorithm to show this data processing.

Suggested answer

```
Read card NUMBER
if card is stolen then END
if purchase amount is greater than allowed to spend then END
output the authorisation code
END
```

24.2 Paper B

1   State **four** problems which may arise when converting a paper-based office to an electronic office.

2   State **two** household appliances which contain a microprocessor and describe the purpose of the microprocessor in each appliance.

3   (a) Explain what is meant by a computer virus.

      (b) Outline **two** precautions that a computer systems manager can take to reduce the effects of viruses.

4   (a) What is the purpose of a graphical user interface?

      (b) Why is using a graphical user interface more popular than typing in command lines?

      (c) Describe **three** tasks that an operating system does for the user.

5   A large suite of software is on a desktop computer. Describe **three** advantages of installing the software from CD-ROM rather than from floppy disk.

6   A student has decided to use the wide area network (Internet) to research information for science coursework.

      (a) State **two** examples of information, other than plain text and pictures, that the student can find on the Internet.

      (b) Describe how information from the Internet can be included in a piece of coursework.

      (c) Explain how checksums are used in the transfer of data.

7   A hotel wants to change from a manual booking system to a computerised one.

      (a) Describe why first a feasibility study should be carried out.

      (b) Describe, using a data flow diagram or otherwise, the flow of data in the manual booking system.

      (c) Describe **two** benefits of using top-down design to develop this computer system.

8   This algorithm grades candidates on marks out of ten.

```
1  input a Mark
2     case Mark of
3        0, 1, 2, 3      : Grade = Fail
4              4, 5      : Grade = Pass
5              6, 7      : Grade = Merit
6        8, 9, 10        : Grade = Distinction
7     otherwise Mark = –1
8  endcase
```

CS

9 if **Mark** = −1 then
10   print 'Not a valid mark'
11 else output **Grade**, 'Grade'

(a) Dry run the algorithm for each of the following data and complete the table.

INPUT	OUTPUT
0	
5	
99	

(b) Write down **two** instructions which could be inserted between lines 1 and 2 to allow the algorithm to deal with marks out of 100.

| CS | 9 |

(a) The systems flowchart represents a batch update of a payroll master file stored on magnetic tape. Using the following words label the diagram below. You may assume that the transaction file has been validated.

error report   new master file   old master file
sort   sorted transactions   update

(b) Describe the consequences of systems failure of
   (i) a real-time air traffic control system
   (ii) the batch update of a sequential payroll master file.

10 The following spreadsheet shows a student's expenses for four weeks.

	A	B	C	D	E	F
1	ITEMS	WEEK 1	WEEK 2	WEEK 3	WEEK 4	TOTAL
2	TRAVEL	4.50	3.60	1.80	6.30	
3	FOOD	29.00	32.00	25.00	33.00	
4	CLOTHES				15.00	
5	STATIONERY	5.20				
6	LEISURE	39.00	42.00	26.00	35.00	
7	TELEPHONE	2.20	2.50	2.50	2.50	

(a) Write down a cell reference which contains
   (i) a label
   (ii) a value.
(b) Write a formula that should be inserted into **F2** to calculate the total expenditure on travel for these four weeks.
(c) Describe how the formula in **F2** can be replicated to calculate the total expenditure for each item.
(d) Write a formula that should be inserted into **F8** to calculate the total expenditure for all items.
(e) A pie chart is needed to show the percentage spent on each item over the four weeks. On the spreadsheet, shade the cells needed to produce this chart.

11 A publisher uses a database to keep details of the books in stock. Part of the database is shown below.

CATNO	TITLE	AUTHOR	PUBLISHED	SALES
B295	Buying a Boat	Smart I	1995	1437
I392	The Internet	Cheung L	1992	5612
C499	Your Computer	Patel M	1997	2172
S500	Swimming	Winship P	2000	475
M401	Multimedia	Sutton D	2001	1762
A301	Antique Cars	Brown M	2001	46

(a) State the name of a field that contains
   (i) numeric data
   (ii) alphanumeric data.
(b) (i) State the name of the field that should be used as the key field.
   (ii) Explain the purpose of a key field.
(c) The book file is to be linked to a customer file. Explain the contents of another field needed to link both files.
(d) The records are sorted into descending order of **SALES**. The following search condition is then input.
   (SALES < 3000) AND **(PUBLISHED** < 1998)

CS

Write down the output using only the **CATNO** field in the correct sorted order.

(e) State **three** validation checks that could be done on the **CATNO** field.

12 Employees of a shop are entitled to a discount of 10% on the value of goods bought from the shop. However, if an employee has worked at the shop for five or more years they are entitled to a discount of 20%. Only employees are allowed discounts. The discount on electrical goods is fixed at 10%.

Using pseudocode or otherwise, write an algorithm which will determine what discount applies when any person buys an item.

24.3 Paper C

CS 1 Explain, using examples, the meaning of these computer terms.
   (a) data logging
   (b) check digit
   (c) serial access
   (d) assembler
   (e) handshaking

CS 2 State **three** ways that Data Protection Rules protect personal data.

3 (a) State **two** sensors that could be used in a microprocessor-controlled washing machine.
   (b) Describe how the data collected by the sensors would be used by the control program.

4 (a) State **two** tasks done by robots on the production line in a car factory.
   (b) Describe how a robot is able to move around the factory without bumping into anything.
   (c) State **two** effects on factory workers of robots being used in the manufacturing of cars.

CS 5 (a) Explain why buffers are needed.
   (b) Give a reason for increasing the size of a buffer.
   (c) Explain the purpose of interrupts in the transmission of data to a printer.

6 The diagram shows part of a directory structure displayed by a windows-based operating system.

   (a) Name
       (i) a root directory
       (ii) a subdirectory.
   (b) Describe what happens to a floppy disk when it is formatted.
   (c) State **three** tasks, other than formatting, that an operating system will do for a user.

7 A hotel has decided to invest in a new computer system.
   (a) State **three** tasks in the design of this new system.
   (b) State **two** stages in the implementation of the new system.
   (c) State **two** items of user documentation that should be provided.

8 A database contains data about items that have been ordered from suppliers.

SUPPLIER	CODE	DELIVERY DATE	PRICE($)
A012	2146	28/09/02	44.99
C035	3724	30/09/02	249.5
M018	5613	05/10/02	98.15
L047	5613	11/10/02	102.75
P029	7215	17/10/02	127.5
R016	4639	19/10/02	22.89

(a) State a field that only contains numeric data.

(b) Describe **two** validation checks that could be made on the DELIVERY DATE.

(c) The following search condition is input.

(**CODE** = 5613) AND (**PRICE($)** < 100).

Write down the output using only the SUPPLIER field.

(d) Write down a search condition that will search for all items with a price more than $50 that will be delivered in October.

9 Read this algorithm.

```
set Total_1 to zero
set Total_2 to zero
set Counter to one
while Counter < eight
    Counter = Counter + 1
    input Number
    if Number > zero then Total_1 = Total_1 + Number
    if Number < zero then Total_2 = Total_2 + Number
endwhile
output Total_1
output Total_2
```

(a) Write down the output if the following set of numbers are input.
4, 1, –3, 2, –5, 0, 6

(b) Modify the algorithm so that it will accept any number of numbers, the input is terminated by a rogue value and the output is the **Total** of all the numbers input except the rogue value.

10 A tourist information centre has its own website.

(a) Explain the purpose of the modem and the Internet Service Provider (ISP) that the centre uses.

(b) Describe **two** ways that information about visitors to the website and their requirements could be collected by the web pages.

CS

CS

CS

11 Describe how an expert system would identify types of plants.

12 (a) State **two** causes of systems failure.

CS

(b) State **two** ways the data can be protected against systems failure.

13 A computer is used to control the traffic at a busy road junction.

(a) State an input device that should be used.

(b) State an output device that could be used.

(c) Describe the processing done by the computer to control the output

CS

device.

14 A company uses the following systems flowchart for online order processing and invoicing.

Write the terms from the list below into the correct symbols in the flowchart. One term has been done for you.

customer orders   invalid orders
invoices   order entry
order file   stock file
update process   validation process

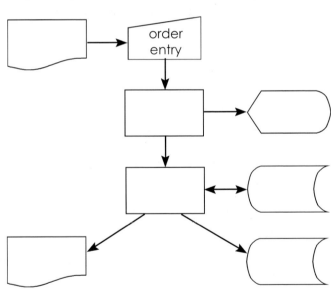

24.4 Paper D

1   Which **two** items contain personal data?

car park ticket	credit card	digital clock
keyboard	pupil record	remote control

Suggested answers

- ◆   pupil record
- ◆   credit card

2   Match the software with its use.

Software	Use
Presentation graphics	recording data in a science experiment
Word processor	preparing a talk to show how a computer works
Spreadsheet	writing letters to parents
Database	keeping school tuck shop accounts
Desktop publishing	storing pupil records
Measuring program	producing the school magazine

Suggested answers

Software	Use
Presentation graphics	preparing a talk to show how a computer works
Word processor	writing letters to parents
Spreadsheet	keeping school tuck shop accounts
Database	storing pupil records
Desktop publishing	producing the school magazine
Measuring program	recording data in a science experiment

3   Give **two** ways in which a hard disk is different from a CD-ROM.

Suggested answers

Hard disk	CD-ROM
Magnetic	Optical
Read/write	Read only
Usually fixed inside one computer / not portable	Transfer data from one computer to another / portable
Storage capacity now in Gb	Storage capacity limited to 650/700 Mb
Data access speed quicker	Data access speed slower

4   Describe **two** precautions you can take to prevent viruses from entering your computer system.

Suggested answers

- use antivirus software
- use a firewall
- don't use disks from unknown sources
- don't open attachments in emails from unknown sources
- restrict access to wider networks (includes the Internet)

5   (a) Name **two** types of software which could be used in a school's sports department.

     (b) State how each type of software would be used.

Suggested answers

(a) - database
     - spreadsheet
     - presentation
     - word processor
     - DTP
     - data logging
     - imaging

Note: Brand names such as Microsoft Word, Excel, etc., would not *be acceptable answers.*

(b)

Software	Use
Database	Pupil records Attendance registers Sports equipment inventory
Spreadsheet	Sports results League tables
Word processor	Writing reports Preparing lesson notes
Presentation	Preparing lessons / demonstrations
DTP	Producing newspaper / magazine
Data logging	Fitness monitoring
Imaging	Digitise video of performance Analyse technique

Note: These answers are only suggestions and any reasonable / sensible use will be accepted.

6   State **one** advantage and **one** disadvantage of using a laptop computer rather than a desktop computer.

Suggested answers

Advantages	Disadvantages
Do your work where you want / portable	Limited battery use
Bring your laptop to class to take notes	Potential loss of confidentiality / screen can be overlooked in public places
Degree of privacy by keeping it with you	Some people find keyboard / pad difficult to use
	Risk of losing laptop or having it stolen

7   You have been asked to set up a science experiment to measure the rates of cooling of different liquids. You must use a computer to do this. You will need a monitor, keyboard and a mouse to help set up the experiment.

Name **three** other items of hardware or software. For each one you will need to say what it will be used for.

Suggested answers

Hardware/software	Use
Temperature sensor	To record the temperature of the liquid
ADC (Analogue to digital converter)/ data logger	To convert the analogue data into a digital form that can be input to the computer
Spreadsheet / database	Store / analyse the data

8   A school uses a database to store records about its students. Describe a situation where a record on the database would need to be:
(a)   inserted
(b)   deleted
(c)   amended

Suggested answers

(a)   new student joins the school
(b)   student leaves the school
(c)   change of name / address / telephone number

9   (a)   Name **two** household appliances which use computer control.
(b)   Describe **two** ways in which the use of such appliances has influenced people's lifestyles.

Suggested answers

(a) • mobile phone / cell phone
   • heating / air-conditioning system
   • security system / burglar alarm
   • washing machine / dishwasher
   • video recorder / DVD recorder
   • microwave oven
   • camera / digital camera

(b)

Mobile phone/cell phone	Able to stay in touch Carry on business anywhere
Heating/air-conditioning system	Make life more comfortable Able to live in hot / cold climates
Security system/burglar alarm	Enables people to feel secure in their home at night or when they go out
Washing machine/dishwasher	Allows more free time to do other things
Video recorder/DVD recorder	Plan which TV programmes to watch/record.
Microwave oven	Easy meals to prepare quickly Convenient for people who work and don't want always to cook meals
Camera/digital camera	Automatic settings for taking photographs. Digital cameras allow instant viewing to enable the best photo to be taken – especially useful when visiting a special place or event

10 At the end of the school year the head teacher sends a letter home to parents. This letter contains details of their new class teacher. Describe the steps in the production of such a letter using mailmerge.

Suggested answers

   • Prepare standard letter with all details of new class teacher. Insert the field name(s) / blanks where the individual details are to be inserted. Save this file.
   • Use database of pupil records or compile new list of pupil's name, parents' name and address. Save this file.
   • Load the letter file and link it to the names and address file.

11 Most home computer owners use a modem to connect to the Internet using a telephone line.
   (a) Why is a modem needed?
   (b) Give **two** advantages for individuals of using the Internet in the home.

Suggested answers

(a) The modem converts / changes the digital signals of the computer into analogue signals, which can be sent over the telephone line. Similarly, the modem converts the analogue signals received into digital signals, which the computer can understand.

(b) ◆ email

◆ software downloads / upgrades

◆ shopping

◆ search engines

◆ access to information / newsgroups / chat rooms

◆ banking / finance

Note: You will need to give more details than just the applications listed.

12 (a) Employees in a school office use computers for long periods of time.
(i) Describe **one** health problem which can be caused by such use.
(ii) Describe **one** way in which this might be prevented.

(b) The employees print a lot of copies of the same documents. Give **two** reasons why they should use a laser printer rather than an inkjet printer.

Suggested answers

(a) (i) ◆ repetitive strain injury

◆ eyestrain / headaches

◆ backache

(ii) *repetitive strain injury* – good keyboard design / keyboard position / wrist guards / frequent breaks
eyestrain / headaches – frequent breaks / look away from the screen at frequent intervals / regular eye checks at the optician's / suitable display units must be used / suitable lighting
backache – use adjustable chair / foot rest / regular breaks / adequate sized desk and other furniture

Note: Your answer in this part must *relate to the answer you gave in part (i).*

(b) ◆ cost of printing (running cost lower for a laser printer)

◆ quality of printing (quality higher for a laser printer)

◆ speed (laser printer is faster)

13 A school's student record system is on a completely separate computer network (the 'Admin' network) to the network the students use (the 'Curriculum' network).

The school is buying a computer for the staff workroom. Discuss the advantages and disadvantages of connecting to each network.

Suggested answers

Admin network

Advantages	Disadvantages
Staff able to access pupil records	More users will slow down access time for office staff
Staff able to write reports	Without proper access controls teachers could 'hack' into admin files with serious consequences
Staff can use school management information system to check attendance	

Curriculum network

Advantages	Disadvantages
Teachers and pupils can share work over the network	Pupils have the opportunity to hack into the teachers' work
Teachers can mark work and return to pupils electronically	If connection to both networks, pupils could hack into admin network

Note: These answers are only suggestions – any reasonable or sensible advantage/disadvantage will be accepted.

24.5 Paper E

1   Which are input devices?

> monitor   plotter   printer
> scanner   speaker   touchpad

2   Which **two** items are used to store personal data?

> customer database graphics tablet   magnetic strip on a credit card
> product bar code   a ROM chip   sensor

3   Which **two** items are used to connect computers to the Internet?

> ISDN link   keyboard   MIDI
> modem   monitor   RAM

4   Complete each sentence below using one item from the list.

> analysis   data logging   encryption
> a flowchart   hacking   implementation
> a password   a virus   the world wide web

Interviewing people about a system is _____

Parallel running is a method of _____

You can prevent someone accessing your work by using _____

A program which can damage the contents of a hard disk is called

_____

5   Systems analysts have been employed to computerise the record keeping of a video rental shop. They will be creating one data file of videos and one of customers.

(a) Which **two** items are produced during the design phase?

> evaluation   existing documents   file structure
> questionnaires   parallel running   screen layouts

(b) The customer file will contain details of what the customer looks like. State **two** input devices which would be suitable for inputting an image of the person into this file.

(c) Which field which would be the best choice as the key field of the video file?

> director's name   video reference number
> video title   rental price

6   Architects use CAD packages to draw designs of houses. List **three** features, other than load, save and print, that you would expect to be included in such a package.

7   Complete the sentences using words from the following list:

> MICR   OMR   RAM   ROM   word processing

(a) School registers are read using _____

    (b) The part of central memory which loses its data when the computer is switched off is called _____

    (c) The software package which allows secretaries to type in letters is called a _____ package.

8   Computers are now widely used in libraries.

    (a) State the input device which is used to enter data about a book when it is borrowed.

    (b) Write down the validation check which would be used to make sure the data had been entered correctly.

    (c) List **two** items of information that library members must type before they can access the Internet.

9   A tennis club is planning to keep members' records on a computer database. New members will fill in an application form and be given a membership number. The form will contain the member's personal details as well as their method of payment.

    (a) Design a screen input form to enter all the details onto the computer.

    (b) All the data except for the membership number can be amended. It is very important that this is copied correctly from the application form. Describe **two** methods of verification which could be used to check it has been entered correctly.

    (c) Describe **two** methods of validation which could be used to make sure that the membership number given is valid.

    (d) The club intends to connect to other local clubs using a wide area network. Some of the members are concerned about this plan because they are frightened that their data may be misused.
        Describe **three** ways in which their data might be misused.

    (e) After the system is designed it must be tested. Describe the **three** types of test data which are used to test a system.

10   Describe **two** ways in which a newly created information system can be implemented and for each way give **one** disadvantage of its use.

11   Describe the **two** types of documentation that are found with newly created information systems. Give reasons why each type is needed.

12   More and more people are using the Internet for home banking and home shopping services. Describe the benefits and limitations for individual people in their everyday lives.

13   The employees of many companies communicate through the use of electronic mail and video conferencing.

    (a) What is meant by video conferencing?

    (b) Describe the advantages and disadvantages of video conferencing when compared with electronic mail.

24.6 Paper F

1 Which **two** items are used to output data from a computer?
digitiser   joystick   keyboard
mouse   robot arm   speaker

2 Which **two** items contain personal data?
burglar alarm   car park ticket   credit card
digital speedometer   library card   remote control

3 Draw **four** lines on the diagram to match the software to its use. One has been done for you

Software	Use
Word processor	accounting
Spreadsheet	room design
Graphics program	storing records
Database	controlling traffic lights
Control program	writing letters

4 Data about pupils is stored in a datafile.
  (a) Give **one** reason why the date of birth is stored and not the age of the pupil.
  (b) Give **one** reason why each record has a record number.
  (c) Give **one** reason why the data for Male or Female is coded M or F.
  (d) Give **one** reason why the data is validated.

5 A floor turtle can use the following instructions:

INSTRUCTION	MEANING
FORWARD n	Move n mm forward
BACKWARD n	Move n mm backward
LEFT t	Turn left t degrees
RIGHT t	Turn right t degrees
PENUP	Lift the pen
PENDOWN	Lower the pen

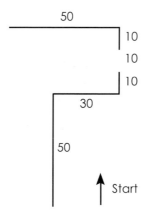

Complete the set of instructions which draw this shape.
    PEN DOWN
    FORWARD 50
    RIGHT 90

6 At the end of a lesson a pupil makes a back-up of the work done on a word processor.
    (a) What is a back-up?
    (b) Why is it made?

7 Give **two** ways computers are used to monitor traffic.

8 Pupil records and school accounts are kept on a computer in the office of the school secretary.
    (a) Select from the list **one** item of hardware and **two** items of software that are required.
            compact disk   database   CAD   data logger
            graphics package   hard disk   spreadsheet
    (b) Give **two** occasions when a pupil's record will need to be altered.
    (c) State **two** ways in which the school accounts can be protected from unauthorised access.

9 One reason for using a computer model is to reduce cost by not having to build the real thing. Give **two** other reasons.

10 Give **two** advantages of using automatic data-logging equipment rather than taking readings manually.

11 A pupil is researching material for a school project. The pupil has a computer which has a CD-ROM drive and access to the Internet.
    (a) Give **one** advantage of using the Internet rather than a CD-ROM.
    (b) Give **one** advantage of using a CD-ROM rather than the Internet.

12 A youth club asks you to create a database of members. State **four** things you would need to consider before creating the database.

13 State **two** disadvantages to you of using a computer to shop from your home.

14 State **two** disadvantages of having an Internet connection at home.

15 Give **two** ways in which a computer password can be kept secure.

16 A computerised robot is learning to travel round a maze.
   (a) State **two** sensors which would be used to detect the wall.
   (b) When the robot detects a wall it will stop. Describe what the robot should be instructed to do to continue through the maze.

17 A computer room contains 20 machines that children use for 40 minutes each day. Give **three** safety measures, with reasons, which should be taken.

18 A school is going to install six computers in its library. Describe how this will affect staff and pupils.

25 Examination questions organised by topic

25.1 Applications of computers

1. Traffic lights are controlled by a microprocessor system. State **two** methods of automatic collection of traffic data.

2. (a) State **two** industrial tasks that make use of robots
   (b) State **two** advantages and **two** disadvantages of using robots in industry.

3. (a) State **one** practical use of a virtual reality system.
   (b) For this virtual reality system state **two** items of special hardware needed.

4. Weather satellites transmit images as coded radio signals to a computer on earth.
   (a) Give **two** ways software could be used to process these images.
   (b) Suggest **two** advantages of using data from satellite systems rather than data from weather stations on the ground for forecasting the weather.

5. An expert system is to be created for medical diagnosis. Explain the steps needed to achieve this.

6. A doctor is planning to store patient records on a computer system.
   (a) State **three** Data Protection Rules that the doctor should obey.
   (b) Describe **two** possible effects if the doctor does not obey the Data Protection Rules.

7. (a) State **two** possible results when hackers gain illegal access into a business computer system.
   (b) Businesses can protect their computer systems from hacking. State **two** ways in which they can do this.

8. A gardener has installed a microprocessor-controlled system in a greenhouse to control the air temperature.
   (a) State **two** advantages of this system to the gardener.
   (b) State a suitable input device and output device.

9 A microprocessor-controlled air-conditioning system has been installed in a museum.
   (a) (i) State a suitable input device.
       (ii) State a suitable output device.
   (b) Describe the feedback loop which maintains the best conditions in the museum.
   (c) State an advantage for the museum owners of having this system installed.

10 The use of computers at work is thought to be linked to some risks to health.
   (a) Suggest **two** such risks.
   (b) Suggest **two** ways in which these risks may be reduced.

11 A hospital database holds confidential personal data.
   (a) State **two** precautions that the hospital should take to prevent unauthorised access to these data.
   (b) Describe how the database would be recovered if it became corrupted.

12 State **three** benefits of using robots in industry.

13 A school has purchased some data-logging equipment.
   (a) Suggest a suitable data-logging task for the school.
   (b) Describe **two** items of special hardware that the data-logging system could use for the task in (a).
   (c) State **two** advantages of using this system.

14 A computer is used in a hospital to monitor and control a patient's condition.
   (a) State an item of data that could be input.
   (b) Describe the processing done by the computer.
   (c) State an output from the system.

15 New cars can be bought on the wide area network (Internet).
   (a) Describe **two** advantages for the customer of using this method for buying a new car.
   (b) (i) Describe the process used on this network for collecting a customer's details.
       (ii) Explain, using examples, how the system could check that the details typed in by the customer are acceptable.
       (iii) A bank credit card must be used to pay for the car. Explain **one** advantage for the customer of this method of payment.

16 Traffic lights are controlled by a computer system.
   (a) State **two** ways that the data about the traffic are collected.
   (b) Describe how the data collected are used to automatically control the sequence of the traffic lights. Include a description of the role of feedback.

25.2 Systems analysis

1   A mail order company has rapidly increased its business. It has reached the
     point where it must consider changing from a manual order processing
     system to a computerised one.
     (a) Discuss how a systems analyst would investigate the problem and
          would propose a solution.
     (b) State **two** possible effects on the staff when a computer system is
          installed.

2   A small business has decided to change from a manual wages system to a
     computerised wages system for producing the employees' pay.
     (a) State **three** stages in the analysis of the existing system.
     (b) State **two** advantages for the business of writing programs instead of
          buying a software package.
     (c) State **two** types of test data that should be used to test the program.
     (d) State **two** items that should be included in the program's
          documentation.

25.3 Problem solution

CS   1   Describe two differences between assemblers and compilers.

     2   This set of instructions can be used to draw shapes.

INSTRUCTION	MEANING
FORWARD n	Move forward n steps
BACKWARD n	Move backward n steps
RIGHT d	Turn clockwise d degrees
LEFT d	Turn anti-clockwise d degrees

The following set of instructions will produce the square below.
          FORWARD 40
          RIGHT 90
          FORWARD 40
          RIGHT 90
          FORWARD 40
          RIGHT 90
          FORWARD 40
          RIGHT 90

Start

     (a) Sketch the shape produced by this set of instructions.
          FORWARD 30
          LEFT 120

```
FORWARD 30
LEFT 120
FORWARD 30
LEFT 120
```

(b) The set of instructions in (a) can be shortened to:

Repeat 3 [Forward 30, Left 120].

Write a shortened set of instructions for the square.

(c) Explain how the instructions for drawing the square can be turned into a procedure to draw a square of any specified side.

CS | 3 Using pseudocode or otherwise, write an algorithm which will accept ten numbers and print out the smallest number.

CS | 4 (a) Explain why a high-level language is translated into machine code.

(b) Explain **one** difference between an interpreter and an assembler.

CS | 5 Read this algorithm.

```
1  set Total to zero
2  input Number
3      for Count is one to Number
4          input Mark
5          add Mark to Total
6      next Count
7  output Total/Number
```

(a) Dry run the algorithm using the following data.

5, 6, 7, 8, 9, 10

(i) Write down the final value of **Total**.

(ii) Write down the value output.

(b) Re-write the algorithm using a **Repeat … Until** structure.

CS | 6 (a) A program has been written for recording the number of hours of sunshine each day and to calculate the average hours of sunshine per day for each month of the year. Three types of data, standard, extreme and abnormal, are to be used to test this program. Give **one** example of each.

(b) State **two** benefits of writing this program using top-down design.

(c) Describe **three** features of the documentation that would be needed for modifying the program in the future.

CS | 7 Using pseudocode or otherwise, write an algorithm which will take infor-mation about each transaction at a supermarket till, calculate and output

◆   the number of sales,

◆   the number of refunds,

◆   the total amount of money in the till.

CS | **8** An algorithm is needed to input the heights of 15 students in centimetres and print out the height of the tallest student in metres and centimetres. Write a detailed algorithm to do this.

CS | **9** (a) State **two** advantages of using a high-level language rather than a low-level language for writing programs.
(b) Explain the difference between a compiler and an interpreter.

CS | **10** The following set of instructions can be used to control a robot which moves heavy boxes.

INSTRUCTION	MEANING
FORWARD n	Move forward n steps
BACKWARD n	Move backward n steps
RIGHT d	Turn clockwise d degrees
LEFT d	Turn anti-clockwise d degrees
UP n	Move the robot's arms up n cm
DOWN n	Move the robot's arms down n cm

The following set of instructions moves the robot forward 20 steps, turns the robot 90° anti-clockwise and moves the arms up 40 cm.

    FORWARD 20
    LEFT 90
    UP 40

(a) Write **three** more instructions so that the robot will return to its original position.
(b) A procedure (subroutine) called BELT exists to take one box and put it on a conveyor belt. Write an algorithm, using this procedure, to put 50 boxes on the conveyor belt.

25.4 Software and data organisation

1 A software package is used to design a multimedia presentation for a tourist information centre.
(a) Describe how part of a large image on paper may be included in the presentation.
(b) Give **two** types of output, other than text, that you would expect to see in a multimedia presentation.
(c) State how the data is protected against accidental corruption.

2 The spreadsheet chart shows details of items sold in a shop during one day. The day is divided into three time intervals: morning, afternoon and evening.

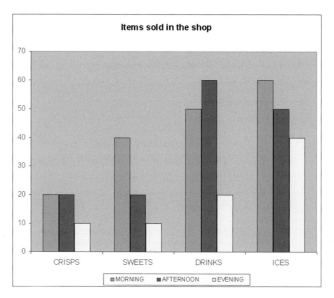

(a) On the spreadsheet, shade the cells that must be used to create this chart.

	A	B	C	D	E	F
1	ITEM	MORNING	AFTERNOON	EVENING	PRICE($)	SALES($)
2	CRISPS	20	20	10	20	1000
3	SWEETS	40	20	10	20	
4	DRINKS	50	60	20	20	
5	ICES	60	50	40	10	
6	TOTAL					

(b) A formula has been put into cell **F2** to calculate the amount of money taken for CRISPS during one day. Describe how this formula could be used to calculate the sales of other items automatically.

(c) Write down a formula that could be put in cell **F6** to calculate the SALES($) for this day

(d) The data for the sales of CHOCOLATE need to be inserted between rows 3 and 4. Describe how this change would be made to the spreadsheet.

3 A database contains a file of houses that are currently for sale.

CODE	TYPE	BEDROOMS	NAME	PRICE($)
2123	B	2	LEE	85000
3124	A	3	JONES	7000
8125	H	8	HART	100000
2126	A	2	PHILLIPS	50000
3127	B	3	PATEL	80000
2128	H	2	CAMERON	60000

(a) Which field in the file should be used as a key field?

(b) Describe **two** validation checks that should be made on the data as new houses are entered into the file.

(c) State **three** more fields that could be included in this file.

(d) State **two** reasons why the data in the **TYPE** field have been coded

(e) The following search condition is input.

(**TYPE** = "B") or (**BEDROOMS** < 4)

Write down the output using only the **CODE** field.

(f) Write down a set of steps to search for all the three-bedroomed houses which are priced at $80,000 or more.

(g) A second file contains details of possible buyers. Describe how this second file can be used with the first file.

4 The following spreadsheet shows the usage (in hours) of the Internet during one week compared with the same week the previous year.

	A	B	C	D	E
1		1999 hours	2000 hours	Change	% Change
2	Monday	25	30	5	
3	Tuesday	48	64		
4	Wednesda	30	15		
5	Thursday	20	40		
6	Friday	70	80		
7					

(a) Write down a cell which should contain (i) a value, (ii) a formula.

(b) An extra column has been added to show the %Change from 1999 to 2000.

%Change = Change*100/(1999 hours)

Write a formula that should be inserted into **E2** to calculate the %Change. Explain how the contents of **E2** can be displayed to show one decimal place.

(c) A labelled bar chart is needed to compare the hours for this week in 1999 and in 2000. On the spreadsheet, shade the cells needed to produce this chart.

5 A garage uses a database to keep details of the cars in stock. Part of the database is shown below.

REF	MAKE	DOORS	YEAR
F214	FORD	3	1998
R317	RENAULT	4	1995
F219	FORD	5	1997
M412	MAZDA	5	1994
T517	TOYOTA	3	1996
C615	CITROEN	4	1995

    (a) State the names of the fields that contain (i) numeric data, (ii) alphabetic data.

    (b) Suggest **two** additional fields that could usefully be added to this database.

    (c) The following search condition is input

        (**REF** contains "M") OR (**YEAR**>1996)

    Write down the output using only the **REF** field

    (d) The records need to be sorted into the key field order. State which field would be used as the key field and give a reason why.

    (e) The database is sorted into descending order on the **YEAR** field. Write down the output using only the **REF** field.

CS	**6**

Errors can occur in data when it is being transmitted. A zero can be changed to a one and a one can be changed to a zero.

A method of checking the data is to write 1 in bit position 7 if there is an odd number of 1s in the other 7 bits, otherwise write 0 in bit position 7. For example the following bit pattern has a 1 in bit position 7 as the other bits contain an odd number of 1s.

Bit position →

7	6	5	4	3	2	1	0
1	0	0	1	1	1	0	0

Data →

(a) Complete the bit pattern below by writing the bit which should be in position 7.

Bit position →

7	6	5	4	3	2	1	0
	1	0	1	1	1	0	0

(b) In order to give a better chance of errors being discovered, a block of data can have vertical as well as horizontal checks. Complete the following table by inserting the bits that should be on the bottom row.

Bit position →

7	6	5	4	3	2	1	0
1	0	1	0	0	0	0	0
1	0	0	1	1	1	0	0
1	1	1	1	1	1	1	1
0	1	0	1	0	1	0	1
0	0	0	0	1	1	0	0
0	0	0	0	1	1	0	0
		0	1	0			

(c) Suggest a reason why a bit could have changed when the data was transmitted.

CS 7 A burglar alarm system is controlled by a microprocessor. Data is collected by sensors. Each sensor gives an input to the microprocessor of 0 when no burglar is detected and 1 when a burglar is detected. The inputs are stored as shown.

1	1	0	1	0	0	0	0
alarm	output 2	door 1	door 2	window 1	window 2	... not in use ...	

OUTPUT | INPUT

(a) Describe what has happened to create this pattern.
(b) Write down a bit pattern that could be set when a burglar enters through window 1.
(c) (i) State **one** use of output 2.
(ii) The sensors for the four inputs shown are simple switches. State one further type of suitable sensor.

8 (a) State **three** items that could be imported into a word-processed document.
(b) Describe **two** ways of importing these items into a word-processed document.

CS 9 A school is to use a data-logging system to monitor weather conditions for a week.
(a) (i) Suggest a suitable time interval for collecting the temperature data.
(ii) Give a reason for your suggestion in (i).
(b) To collect the temperature data a thermometer is used. State **two** other sensors which should be included in the system.
(c) Describe **three** features of the software used with this system.
(d) Describe how the results of the monitoring could be compared with those of the previous week

10 The email address for an employee of a company selling cars has the following format:

person@company.co.uk

(a) Write down the email address for a person named Ben working at a UK company called Webcars.
(b) State **one** advantage and **one** disadvantage for the company of using email for communicating with its customers.

11 A mail order company holds details of items on a stock file. Each stock record consists of a four-character code, a description of the item, the

number in stock, the reorder level and the date of the last order.

	Field Name	Data Type
	ITEM CODE	Number
	DESCRIPTION	Text
	NUMBER IN STOCK	Number
	REORDER LEVEL	Number
	DATE OF ORDER	Date / Time

(a) Which field should be used as a key field?

(b) State the type of file access needed.

(c) The data are to be held in *fixed-length* records. Give **one** advantage and **one** disadvantage of using fixed-length records.

(d) A customer telephones to place an order. Describe how the order-processing system would check to see if an item is out of stock.

12 Describe **two** ways that a scanner could be used to transfer paper-based documents to files stored on a computer.

13 The following spreadsheet shows the results of two tests. The cells D2:D6 each contain a formula.

	A	B	C	D	E
1		TEST 1 out of 100	TEST 2 out of 100	AVG Mark	Pass
2	M Davies	82	68	75	YES
3	J Griffiths	48	72		NO
4	S Harrison	98	98		YES
5	M Khan	88	62		YES
6	I Patel	70	80		YES

(a) Write down a **cell** which should contain
   (i) a label
   (ii) a number.

(b) Suggest a formula that could be in D2 to calculate the average mark.

(c) Describe how the formula in D2 can be copied into the range of cells D3:D6

(d) Describe how the results for TEST 1 can be displayed in descending order.

(e) A bar chart is needed to compare the average marks for each student. Write down the range of cells needed to produce this chart.

14 Part of a holiday file is shown below.

BOOKING NO	MEALS	NIGHTS	HOTEL	PRICE($)
BK0042	RO	7	REGENT	250
BK0043	FB	5	SAVOY	400
BK0044	HB	6	BROWNS	350
BK0046	FB	7	SEAVIEW	375
BK0048	BB	10	HILL TOP	295
BK0050	HB	7	VALLEY	475

The following codes represent the meals.

MEALS RO – room only

BB – bed and breakfast

HB – half board

FB – full board

(a) Complete the table below to show the data type and field size for each field.

FIELD NAME	DATA TYPE	FIELD SIZE
BOOKING NO		
MEALS		
NIGHTS		
HOTEL		
PRICE($)		

(b) State **two** reasons why the MEALS data have been coded.

(c) Suggest **two** more fields that could be used in this file.

(d) The following search condition is input

(MEALS = "RO") OR (PRICE($) > 350)

(i) Write down the output using the BOOKING NO only.

(ii) Write a similar search condition which will display the holidays that are more than 7 nights and cost $450 or more.

(e) Describe the processing and output when a customer books a holiday.

25.5 Hardware, systems and communications

1 State **one** storage device used to store data permanently and describe how these data are stored.

CS 2 (a) A network has more than one printer attached to it. Explain how the network operating system is able to send a user's document to the correct printer.

(b) State **three** other file management tasks that a network operating system does for a user.

3 A business uses a wide area network (Internet) for selling holidays and sending email messages to and from its customers.
   (a) Describe **two** advantages for the business of using this network for selling its holidays.
   (b) Describe **two** benefits for the customer of using email to communicate with the business.
   (c) Describe the process used by a customer to access information on this network.
   (d) Payment for the holidays must be made by bank credit card. Explain why some people are unhappy about this method of payment.

CS **4** State **three** tasks that an operating system carries out.

5 Disabled people often need special peripheral devices to access computer systems. Describe **two** such devices.

CS **6** A holiday booking firm uses a remote *mainframe computer*.
   (a) Explain why a mainframe is used rather than a desktop computer.
   (b) Explain what real-time processing occurs during the day.
   (c) Describe **two** tasks that the firm's computer would undertake when the offices are closed.

7 (a) Explain one difference between internal ROM and CD-ROM.
   (b) State **three** differences between magnetic tape and magnetic disk for storing and retrieving data.

8 (a) On the diagram, circle and label

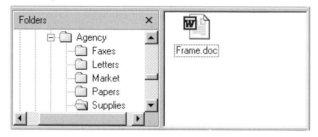

   (i) a directory that includes subdirectories
   (ii) a subdirectory
   (iii) a file.
   (b) Give **one** benefit of using subdirectories.

9 A bank uses a mainframe computer.
   (a) State **three** tasks done by the operating system.
   (b) Describe how the bank's data can be restored after a systems failure.

10 Each evening a travelling salesperson uses a laptop computer and a modem to log on to an Internet Service Provider (ISP) to read their email.

(a) Explain why a modem is needed to communicate with the ISP.
(b) Describe **two** ways that the ISP fileserver will check that the salesperson is an authorised user.
(c) Describe **three** services, other than email and connection to the Internet, that the ISP may offer.
(d) Explain what the Internet is.

25.6 Other topics

CS 1 Explain, using examples where appropriate, the meaning of these computer terms.
(a) magnetic ink character recognition (MICR)
(b) handshaking
(c) polling
(d) batch processing
(e) graphical user interface (GUI)

CS 2 Explain, using examples, the meaning of these computer terms.
(a) multimedia
(b) array
(c) de-skilling
(d) expert system
(e) verification

CS 3 Explain, using examples if appropriate, the meaning of these computer terms.
(a) macro
(b) buffer
(c) file generations

CS 4 Explain, using examples if appropriate, the meaning of the following computer terms.
(a) validation
(b) random access memory (RAM)
(c) job control language
(d) interrupt
(e) stepwise refinement

Glossary of terms

Glossary of terms

A

actuator – a device used to carry out the physical requirements of a computer

algorithm – a sequence of instructions used to solve a given problem

analogue data – data in its original, physical, form

analogue to digital converter (A/D converter) – a device that changes analogue data to digital data so that it can be stored and processed in a computer system

applications software – sets of instructions to the computer that allow the user to do something useful

artificial intelligence – an expert system that can change the rules by which it works according to experience of what has happened previously

assembler – software that is used to translate the instructions written in an assembly language into the computer's machine code

assembly language – a low-level language that is close to the computer's machine code

B

back-up file – a copy of a file of information that is stored somewhere away from the computer and can be used to restore the file if the data is lost

bandwidth – a measurement of how much data can be sent along a communications channel at the same time

barcode – a pattern of parallel black and white lines representing a code number that can be read into a computer by a barcode reader; it is used to identify the goods on which it is printed

batch OS – an operating system in which the data to be processed is collected in batches and is then run at some later more convenient time; the data must not be time sensitive

binary code – the representation of a number in the binary system, which comprises only the digits 0 and 1

Boolean data – data that can only exist in two states and hence can be represented by 0 or 1

buffer – an area of memory outside the processor that allows the temporary storage of data while it is waiting to be used

C

changeover – the process by which a new system replaces an old one; typical methods are direct changeover, phased implementation and parallel running

checksum – a validation technique in which a calculation is done before and after data is sent from one place to another to make sure that it has been received without error

closed system – a computer system or network of computers that has no connections to external systems such as the Internet.

coded data – data that has been changed in some way so that entry and storage in the computer are simplified, e.g. M instead of male and F instead of female

command-based interface – interface between the computer and the user that requires the user to type commands at a prompt supplied by the operating system

compiler – software that translates an entire program written in a high-level language into a computer's machine code before it is run

computer-aided design (CAD) – software that allows design work to be carried out on a computer

computer-aided learning (CAL) – using computers to teach students facts about a particular topic; it can also be used for testing students and automatically producing the results

computer-aided manufacture (CAM) – software that allows the manufacture of items which have been designed using CAD

custom-written software – software that is specially commissioned to carry out a particular task

D

data – values that are stored in the computer; it is not in context and hence is meaningless

data dictionary – a list that stores details of data items in a database

data logging – the collection of data for future processing

data table – a table that lists and defines the purpose and type of each variable used in a computer program

database – a collection of data in a computer system; it normally has two or more files (tables) that can interact with each other so that the need for duplication of data is reduced

data-capture form – a form designed to collect data and then to allow easy entry of the data to the computer

dedicated – something that is designed to do only one thing, e.g. a dedicated microprocessor is used to control a washing machine, a job that it does very well, but it can't do anything else

design – producing the parameters of the solution to a problem, either on paper or using a computer; it is done in the order: output, input, storage, processing

de-skilling – the effect on workers who once needed a particular skill to do a job but who no longer need it because it is has been taken over by new technology

desktop publishing (DTP) – software that can import text and graphics to the computer and can then be used to arrange them on a page

digital data – data in electronic form, suitable for storage on and processing by a computer

digital signature – a means of ensuring that the person who sends an electronic communication is really who they say they are; also known as 'electronic signature'

direct access file – a file in which data is indexed, making access to a specific piece of data very fast

distributed network – a network that does not store all the data and files in one place but distributes them around the different computers on the network

dumb terminal – a workstation that is connected to a central processor as part of a multi-access system and does not do any processing itself

E

electronic signature – a means of ensuring that the person who sends an electronic communication is really who they say they are; also known as digital signature

embedded system – a computer system that is built into a machine, usually to provide a means of control

encryption – making text impossible to read by unauthorised people by changing the letters; before reading the contents must be decrypted

expert system – a computer system that stores facts about a particular topic and can search those facts for information according to a set of rules

F

field – an area of a record that stores a specific piece of data

file – a collection of data covering a particular topic

file directory – an index that allows fast access to the files stored on a computer system

firewall – a stand-alone machine through which external messages must pass before being allowed onto a network to prevent viruses and unauthorised access doing any damage to the full system; the term also refers to software stored in a computer whose job is the same

formatting – the preparation of the surface of a storage medium so that it is ready to accept data; the process results in any previous data being erased

G

graphic – pictorial or other data that cannot be stored in the same way as text and numbers

graphical user interface (GUI) – an interface that uses **w**indows to create a border to the information, **i**cons to represent files, **m**enus to allow users to make choices and a **p**ointer to select choices; hence, sometimes called a **WIMP**

graphics tablet – an input device that allows the user to input a graphic by drawing on paper placed on the surface of the tablet

H

hacking – the unauthorised access to computer systems

handshaking – a process that takes place when a computer is about to communicate with a device to establish rules for the communication

hardware – the physical parts of a computer system

high-level language – a computer programming language that consists of statements that are similar to instructions written in English, which makes it easier for programmers but means it has to be translated for use by the computer

human/computer interface (HCI) – the hardware and software that allow communication between a person and a computer

I

icon – a pictorial symbol on a computer screen that represents a choice of activity

information – data stored in the computer after it has been given a meaning by being written in context

input – data that is put into a computer system or the process of putting data into a system

instruction set – the complete set of instructions that are used by a particular type of central processing unit

integrated software – pieces of software that can communicate with one another and share data without changing its form

integrity of data – the correctness of data during and after processing

interface – the hardware and software that create the connection between the user and the computer or the software being used

Internet – a wide area network whose contents are not controlled that is available to anyone with a computer and modem or other way of connecting to the network

interpreter – translator software that translates a single instruction in a high-level language, and allows it to be run before translating the next instruction

interrupt – a signal sent to the processor from some external device, asking the processor to stop what it is doing and do something for the external device instead

intranet – a privately operated wide area network, like the Internet except that the data content and access to it are controlled

item – a piece of information that is stored in a field

iteration – the process of repeating a sequence of steps

K

key field – a field that is used to identify the record within the file; the item within the key field must be unique

keyboard – input device used to input characters

L

light pen – an input device used to input data through a monitor screen

local area network (LAN) – a network in which the computers are physically close together and are connected by wires (or sometimes using wireless communication)

logical data – data which can only have one of two values; also known as Boolean data

low-level language – computer programming language that consists of binary code, which is easy for the computer to understand but difficult for programmers

M

machine code – the set of all possible instructions available from the electronic design of a particular computer; an example of a low-level language

macro – a small program used to customise a piece of software

magnetic disk – storage medium that can store large amounts of data in a way that allows direct access to the data

magnetic ink – special ink used to print characters so that they can be read by people and computers

magnetic ink character recognition (MICR) – the recognition by a computer of special stylised characters printed in magnetic ink

magnetic stripe – a stripe of magnetic material that stores information about the holder, e.g. on a credit card

magnetic tape – storage medium that is now a bit out of date but is still used to keep back-up files on some systems

mainframe computer – large-scale computer typically used in a large organisation to provide the processing power for all the terminals in a multi-user system

microcomputer – typically a personal computer

microphone – device used to input sound to a computer system

microprocessor – a dedicated device that incorporates all the parts of a processor on a single chip

minicomputer – a computer that is larger than a micro but smaller than a mainframe; typically used to control the checkouts in a supermarket

modem – the hardware device that connects a computer to the telephone network and transforms the computer's digital signals to analogue and the telephone network's analogue signals to digital; the word is an abbreviation of 'modulator/demodulator'

module – the smaller components that remain after a problem has been broken down by the use of top-down design

monitor – a device that shows the output from a system in picture form; output is short-lived, unlike that from a printer

multi-access OS – an operating system that allows one computer that does the processing to

be used by a number of people at different terminals

multimedia package – a set of software that uses many different media to convey information, e.g. sound, graphics, animation

multitasking OS – an operating system that allows the user to imagine that they are using the computer to do a number of different things at the same time; Microsoft Windows is a typical multitasking OS

musical instrument digital interface (MIDI) – a device that provides a communications link between an electronic instrument and a computer so that the sounds can be stored digitally

N

network – a group of computers that are linked together so they can communicate with one another

network OS – an operating system that allows a number of machines to be in communication with each other and to share data

O

object code – the machine code program that has been produced by translating a high-level program or an assembly language program.

objectives of a solution – the list of things that a solution should do that has been agreed between the analyst and the user and will be used during the testing of the solution to decide whether or not the solution works

offline OS – a way of using the computer in which the user or device is not directly connected to the processor

off-the-shelf software – software that has already been written and is available immediately

online OS – a way of using the computer in which the user or the device is directly connected to the processor

operating system software – the set of software that controls the hardware of the computer and provides an interface with the outside world

optical disk – a storage device that stores large amounts of data in a way that can be accessed directly using lasers, rather than magnetically

optical mark reader (OMR) – an input device used to detect marks made in pencil on preprinted forms or documents

output – the results produced by a computer system after processing the input data or the action of reading information from a computer system.

P

password – a code known only by the user that allows the computer to be sure of the identity of the person who is accessing information

peripheral device – any device that can be connected to a computer to perform a useful task, e.g. a keyboard and a printer

physical data – data that exists in the physical world, such as length, area, weight; this data is analogue and is not in the right form for a computer

pixel – the smallest part of a computer graphic image; the pixel is so small that it cannot be seen

plotter – a device used to produce hard copy output of line drawings from a computer

pointing device – a device used to input to the computer by pointing at a particular output on the screen, e.g. a mouse

point-of-sale terminal – a shop till (checkout) connected to the shop's computer system

polling – the process by which a processor in charge of a number of devices keeps in touch with them all by asking each in turn if they have anything new to report

presentation software – software that allows a presentation to be produced using linked screens (or frames) that can be followed in an order; the software will allow the use of animation and sound as well as standard outputs

printer – a device used to produce hard copy output from a computer, usually on paper

priority – if more than one thing needs to be done, each is given a priority so that they can be done in order of importance

privacy of data – some data is confidential and methods, such as passwords and encryption, need to be used to ensure that the wrong people do not see it

process control OS – an operating system that allows a processor to control the use of sensors and actuators in order to influence the physical world

processing – the calculations/comparisons that are performed on input data in a computer system

prototype – a partial solution to a problem that is created so that a particular area of the solution can be tested without reference to the rest of the solution

pseudocode – a method of describing the design of a system

R

random-access memory (RAM) – the part of the computer's memory that stores programs and files while they are being used by the computer; the contents of RAM are lost when the power is turned off

read-only memory (ROM) – that part of the computer's memory that is not erased when the power is turned off

real-time OS – an operating system that processes an input and produces output quickly enough to affect the next input

record – a part of a file that stores data about a particular entity; all records in the file store the same type of data

refreshing – the process of replacing the picture on a monitor so that it is always available and up to date

requirements specification – a list of the necessary hardware and software to put a solution into practice and a list of the wishes of the proposed user of the solution

re-skilling – learning and using a new skill to replace another skill that is no longer needed

resolution – a measurement of the clarity of an image based on the number of pixels used to create the image

S

scanner – a device that allows an image that already exists to be input to the computer so that it can be manipulated using special software

search engine – a program used to help find information on the Internet

security of data – the way data is looked after to make sure that it is not damaged, lost or destroyed, typically by making back-ups of the data

sensor – input device that captures physical data

sequential file – a file that stores data in a logical order, e.g. alphabetically

sequential medium – a storage medium, such as magnetic tape, that stores items one after the other in some sort of order

serial file – a file that stores data in the order in which it was received

smart terminal – a workstation connected to a central processor as part of a multi-access computer system that can do some of its own processing

software – the instructions that make a computer do something useful

source code – the original assembly language program or high-level language program before it is translated into machine code

speaker – a device used to produce sound output from a computer; also called loudspeaker

spreadsheet – software designed to handle numbers and calculations; it is also used for predicting future trends according to rules that govern the numerical data input

stepwise refinement – see 'top-down design'

storage – somewhere to store things so that they are not lost when a computer system is switched off, e.g. the computer's hard disk

structure diagram – a diagram used to show how a problem can be broken down into smaller units that can be considered as separate problems, as in top-down design

subdirectory – an index of files of a particular type

supercomputer – the most powerful type of computer whose extremely fast processing speeds make it useful for applications requiring large amounts of calculation, such as weather forecasting

system flowchart – a diagrammatic representation of the way the hardware and software operate in a system and the way that the files are stored

systems analysis – a standardised set of steps that can be used to analyse a problem and design and implement a solution

systems analyst – the person who is responsible for carrying out the stages of systems analysis on a project

T

technical documentation – a set of detailed descriptions about how a solution was arrived at and how it works; it is intended for someone who needs to develop or maintain the system

test plan – a set of test material designed to test specific parts of a solution

test strategy – a decision made by the systems analyst about where, when, how and by who the eventual solution is to be tested

thermistor – an electronic device that reads temperature

time dependent – a process that must be completed within a specific time

top-down design – the breaking down of a large problem into smaller problems; also called stepwise refinement

touch-sensitive screen – a screen that allows input as well as output; input is accomplished by touching an area of the screen

U

user documentation – a set of detailed descriptions about how to use a system to do something useful

user ID – a unique name or code used to let a computer system know who the user is

V

validation – the checking of data input to a system to ensure that it follows certain rules and is therefore sensible

variable – a value, often in an algorithm, that can take different values at different times

verification – the checking of data input to a system to ensure that it is what is meant to have been input

video conferencing – a conference in which a number of people can all see and hear one another while they are physically separated

video digitiser – a device that turns an analogue picture into a digital one suitable for storing in a computer

virtual reality – an electronic environment that seems real to the user; it is achieved through the design of the input to and output from a computer system and may involve the use of special headgear and gloves

virus – a computer program that is maliciously placed on a computer system with the aim of destroying the files on that system and replicating itself so that it can be transmitted to other systems

virus protection – software that identifies viruses and deals with them by not allowing access or erasing them

W

web page – information stored on a single (scrolling) screen on the Internet as part of a website

website – a collection of web pages, normally on a single theme, on the Internet

website authoring software – software that allows the user to create a website with all the features that they want to include

wide area network (WAN) – a network in which the computers are so far apart that they need to be connected in some other way than simply wiring them together

wizard – a special feature of some software that helps users perform a specific task

word processor – software designed to allow the input of text to a computer

Index